I0486103

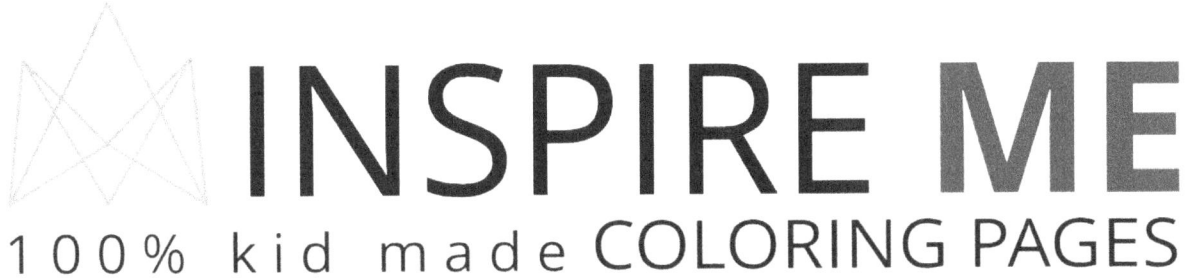

INSPIRE ME
100% kid made COLORING PAGES

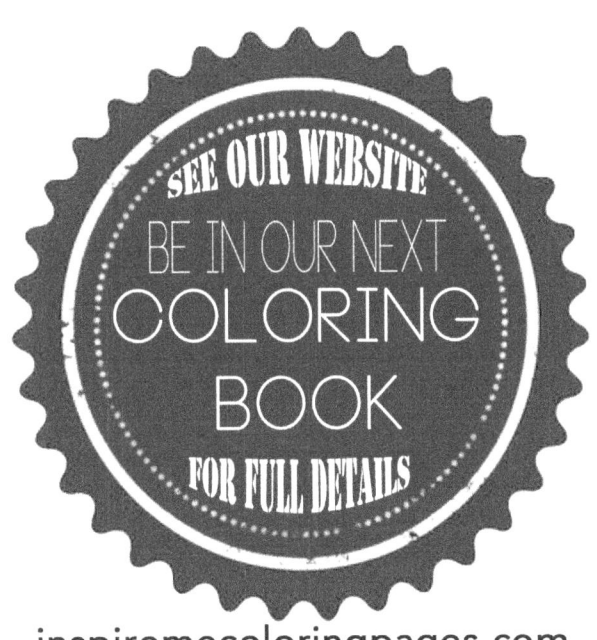

SEE OUR WEBSITE
BE IN OUR NEXT
COLORING
BOOK
FOR FULL DETAILS

inspiremecoloringpages.com

All Illustrations by Foster, Rowan & Emery Weldon

Copyright © 2015 Foster, Rowan & Emery Weldon

All rights reserved.

ISBN: 978-1518766510
ISBN-13: 151876651X

DEDICATION

For artists of all ages.
We hope our coloring book inspires you to draw like a kid again - in awe of the world around you, fearless & uninhibited by the way things "should" be drawn. Please enjoy our original artwork and have fun making something new of your own! We believe God invented each of us to be unique and sharing that uniqueness is one of the greatest joys in life. Enjoy!

PROCEEDS FROM THIS BOOK GO TO THESE AWESOME SCHOOLS:

The Neema Project - neemaproject.org
The Neema Project is an amazing trade school and housing facility for young women in Kitale, Kenya. The students are brave and incredibly strong, beautiful girls from many different backgrounds, most of whom have young children and are unable to find work. The Neema Project seeks to empower students to provide for themselves and their family by teaching valuable life & trade skills.
We would like to sponsor 10 young women as they complete their education.

Windsor Christian Academy - windsorca.org
Our school, Windsor Christian Academy, has been an immense blessing to our family over the past 2 years as we discovered the unique needs of each of our children were not being met at our local public school. WCA not only gives each child a classical education, grounded in the Bible, but they strive to never turn away students for financial reasons. Unfortunately, they have greatly outgrown their current building and are lacking enough space for all of the students who apply.
We would like to help our school build a new building.

Find out more here: inspiremecoloringpages.com

P.S. This is our artwork. We put time and effort and love into each drawing.
Please do not reproduce. For personal use only.

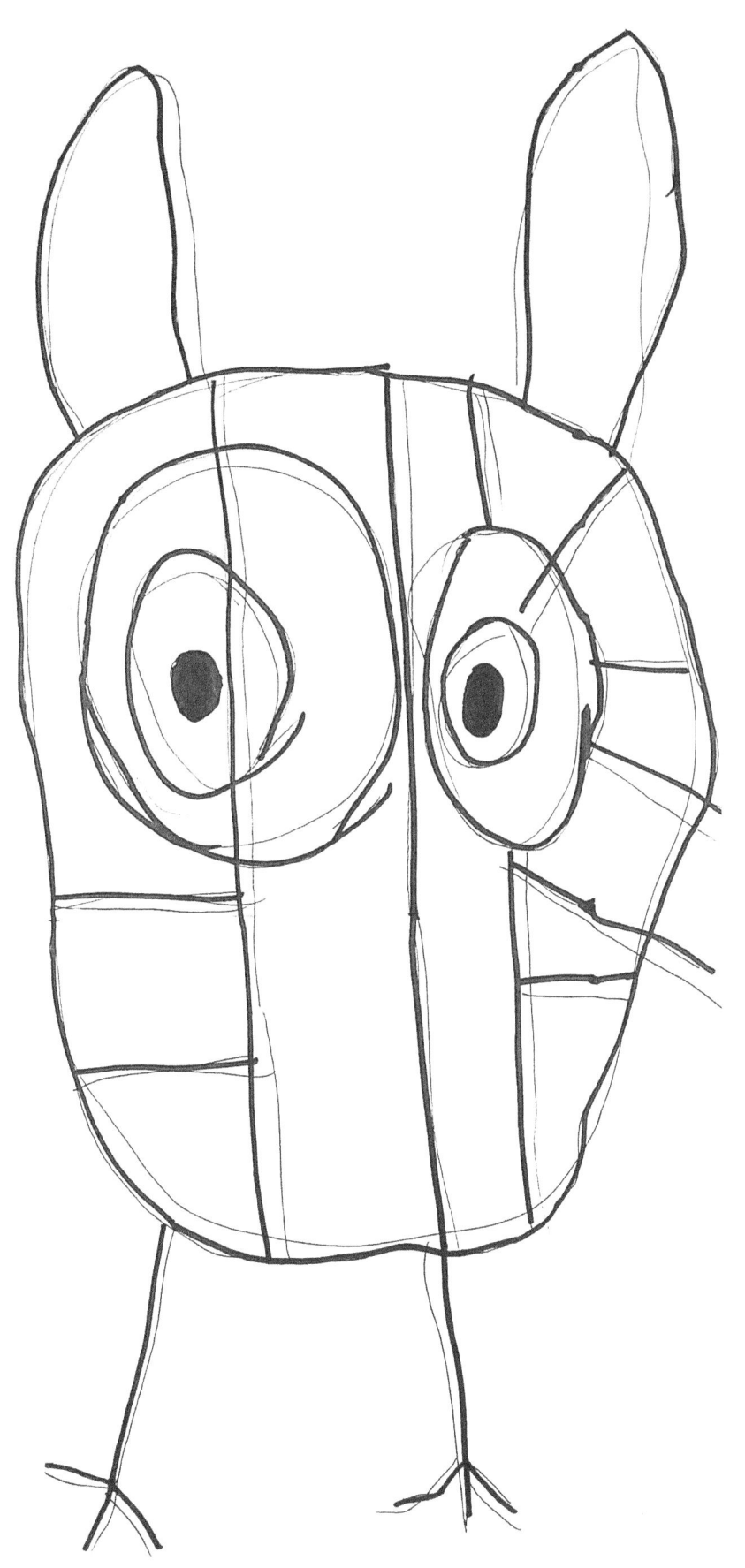

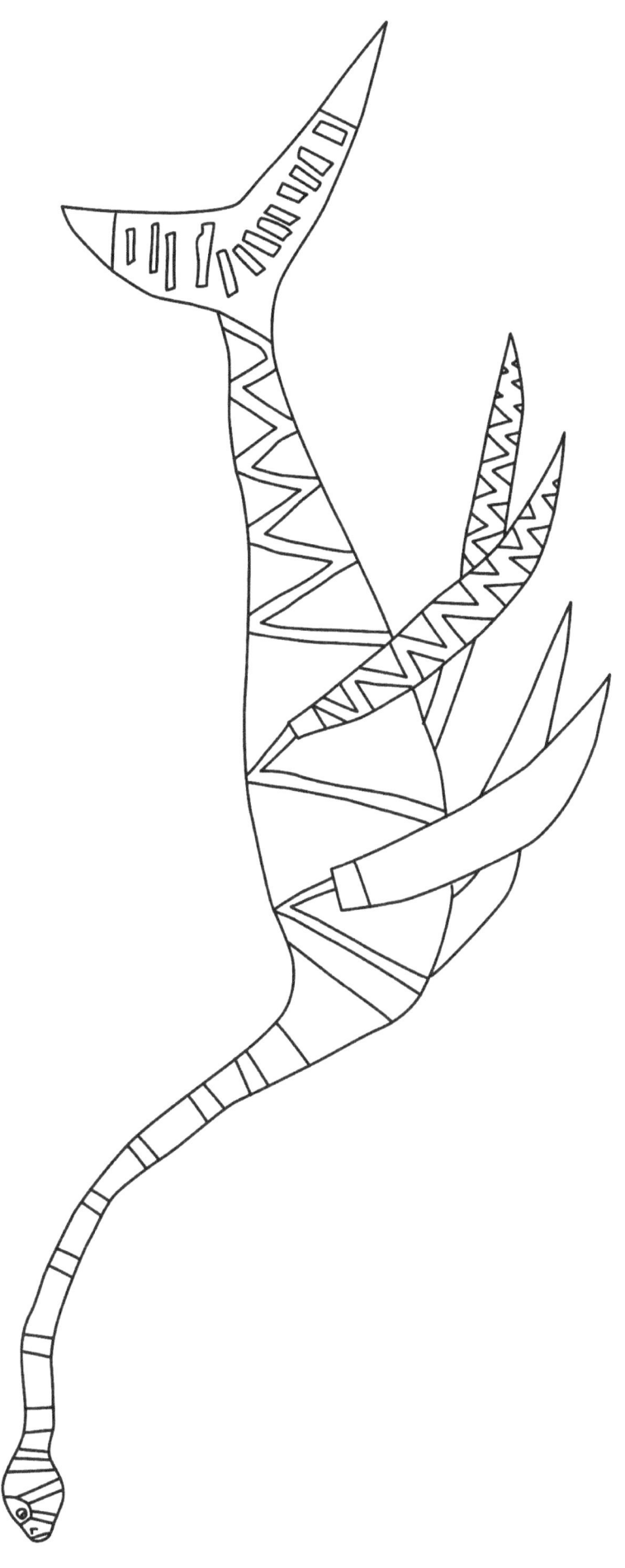

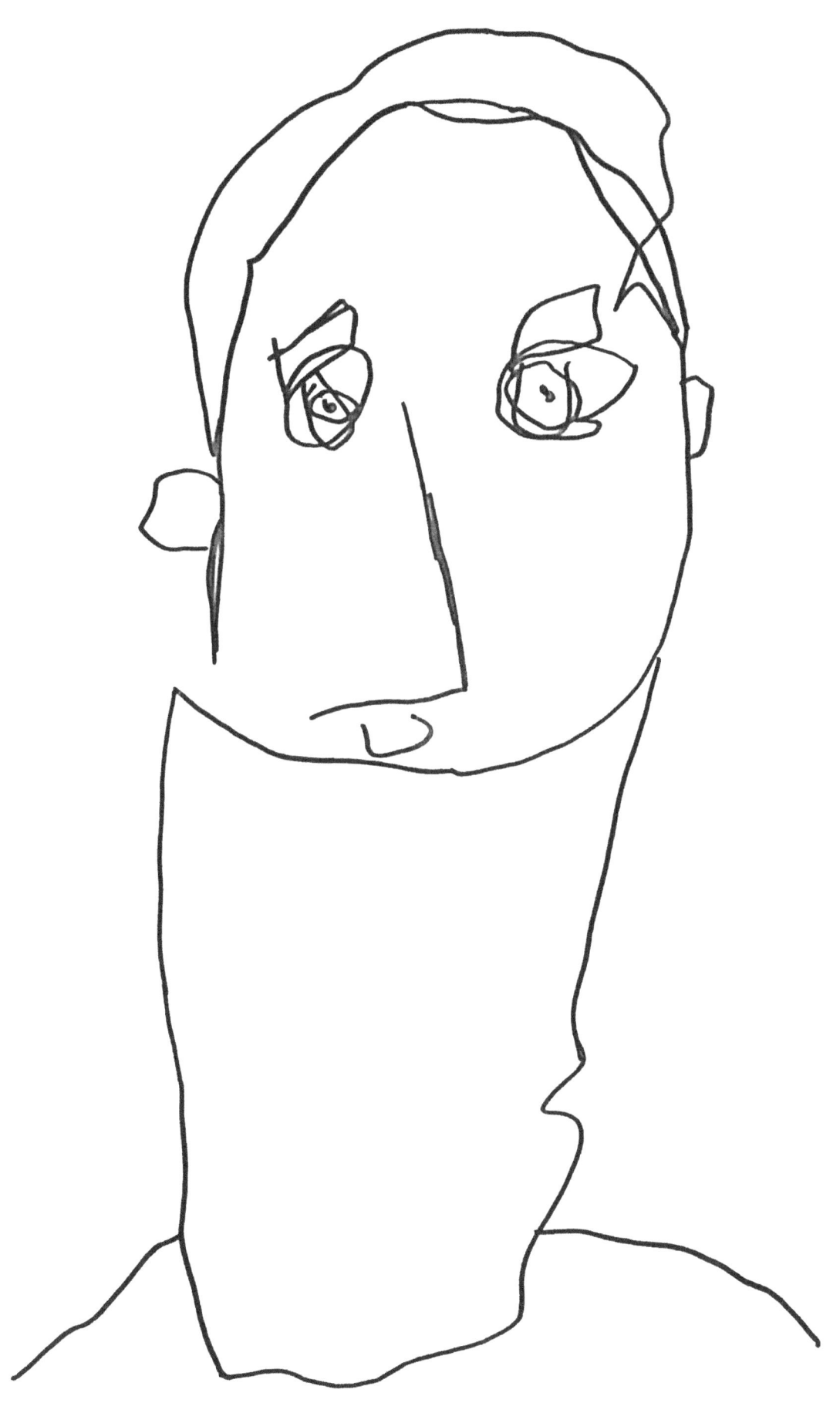

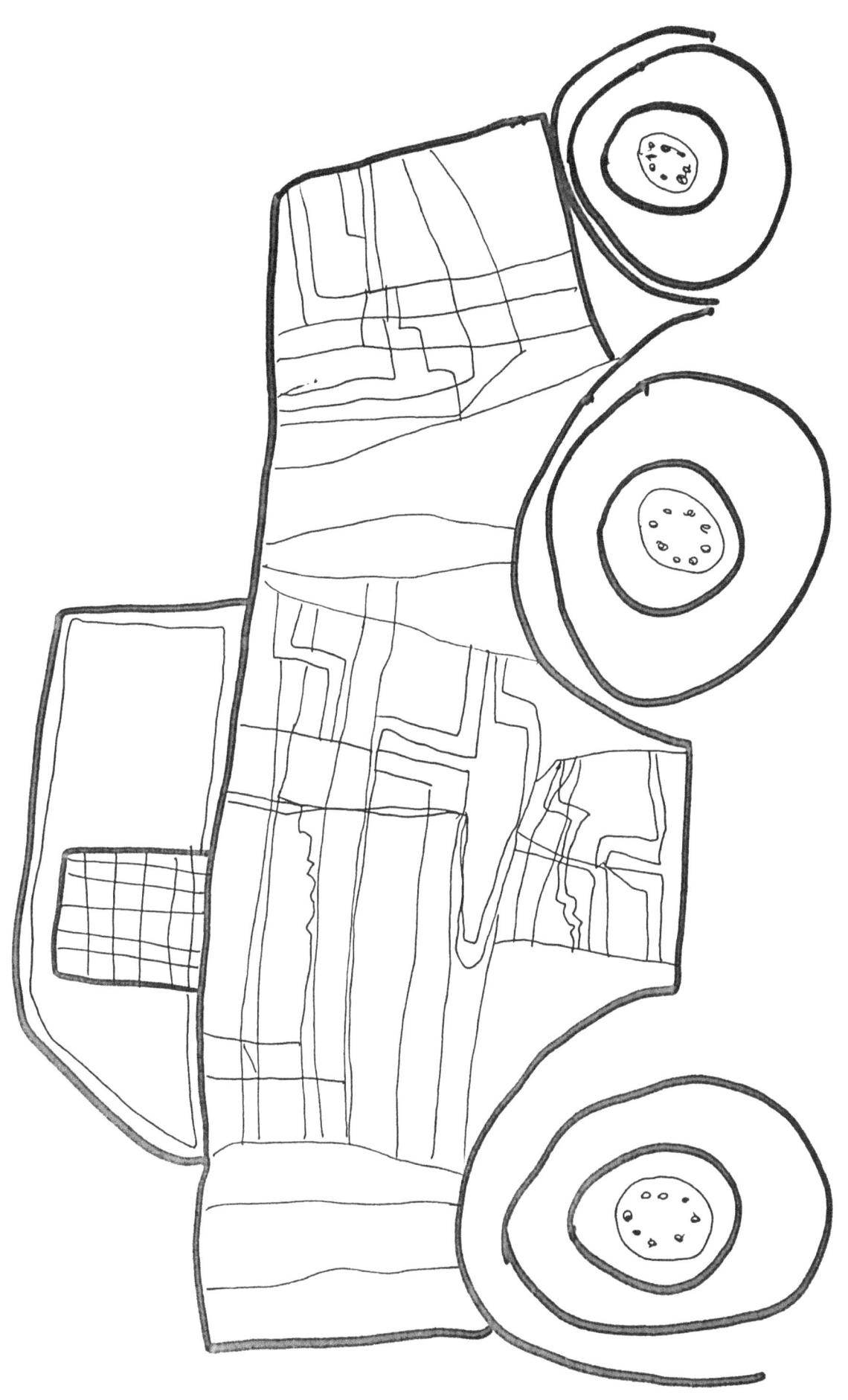

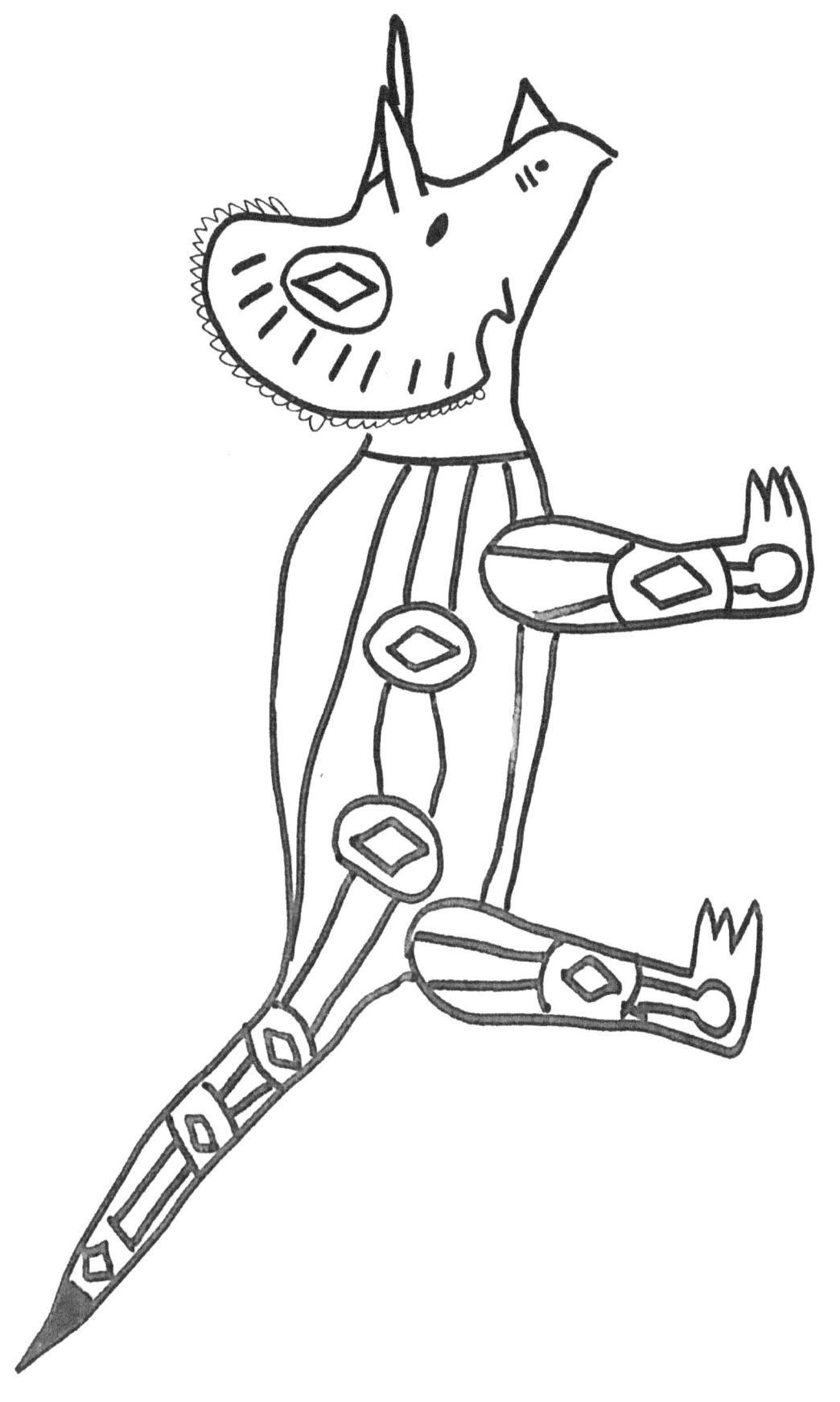

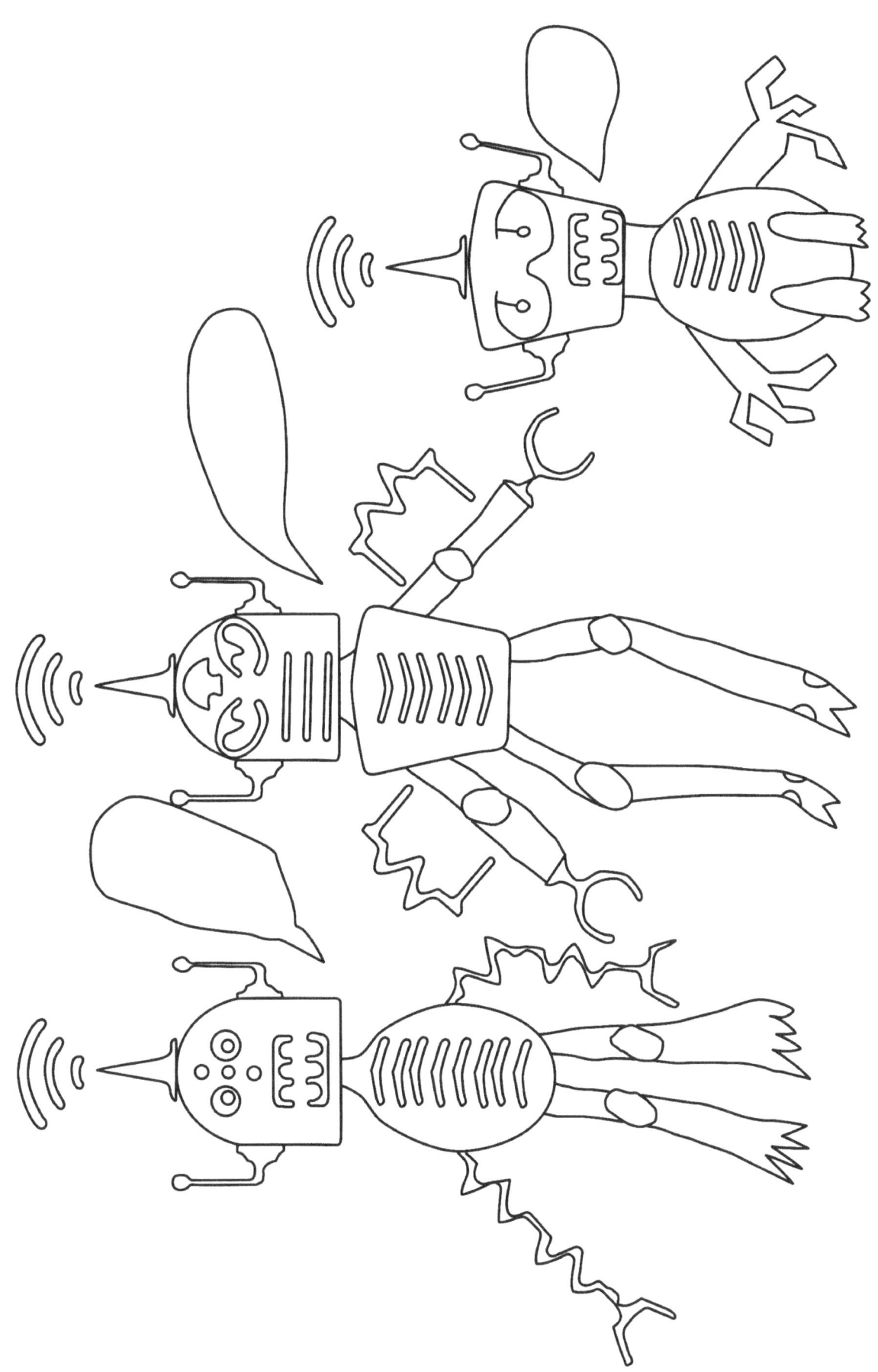

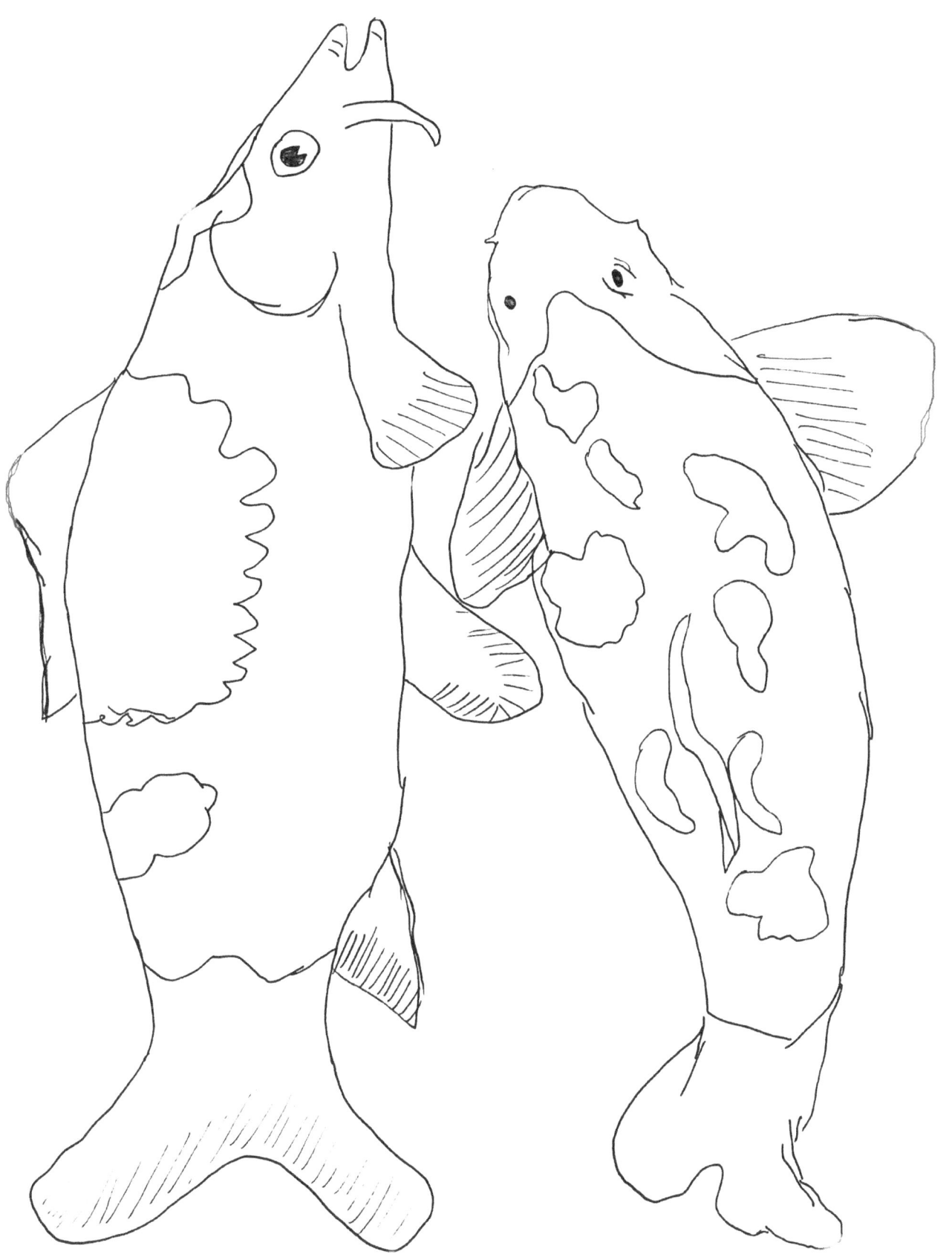

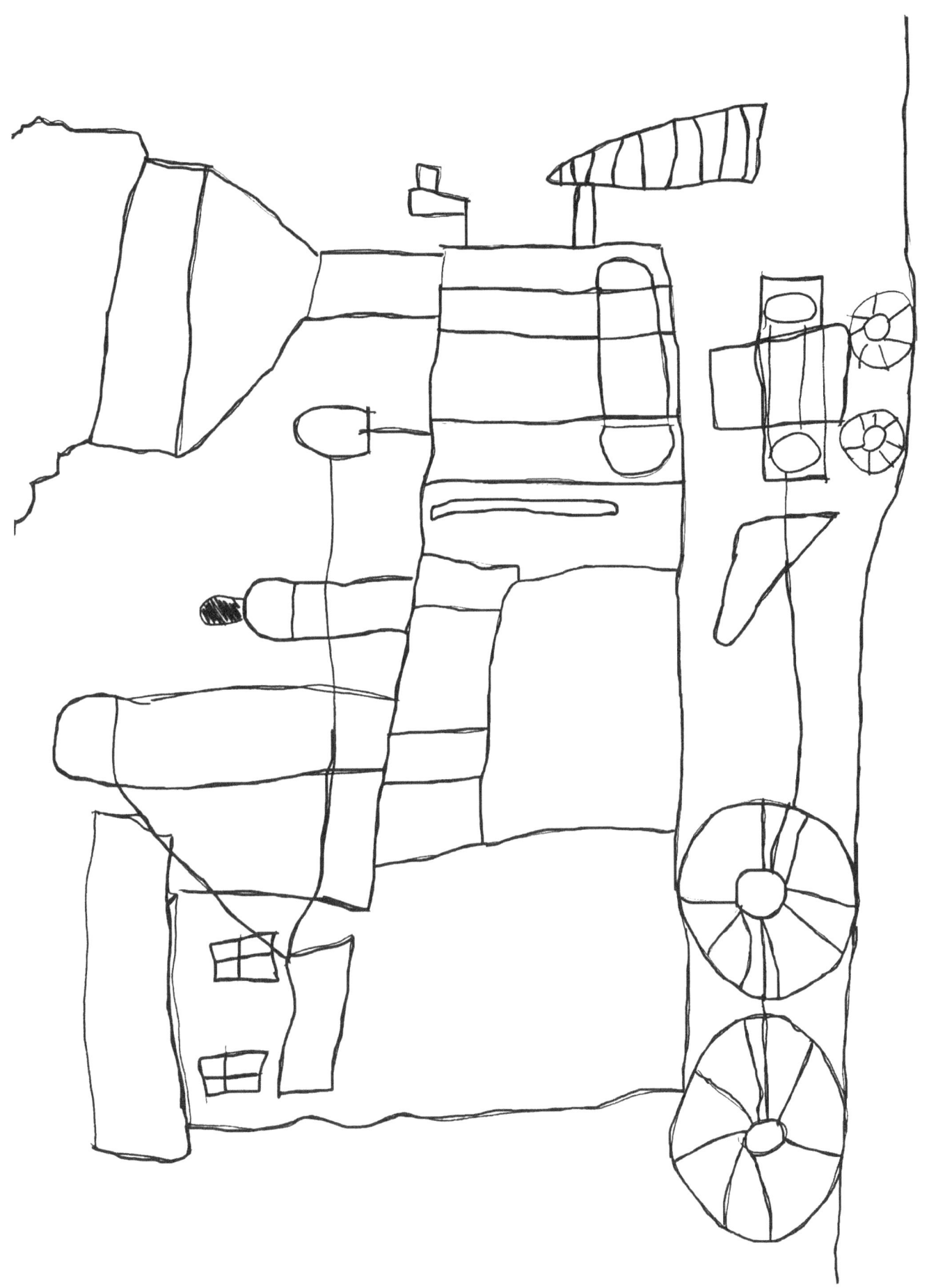

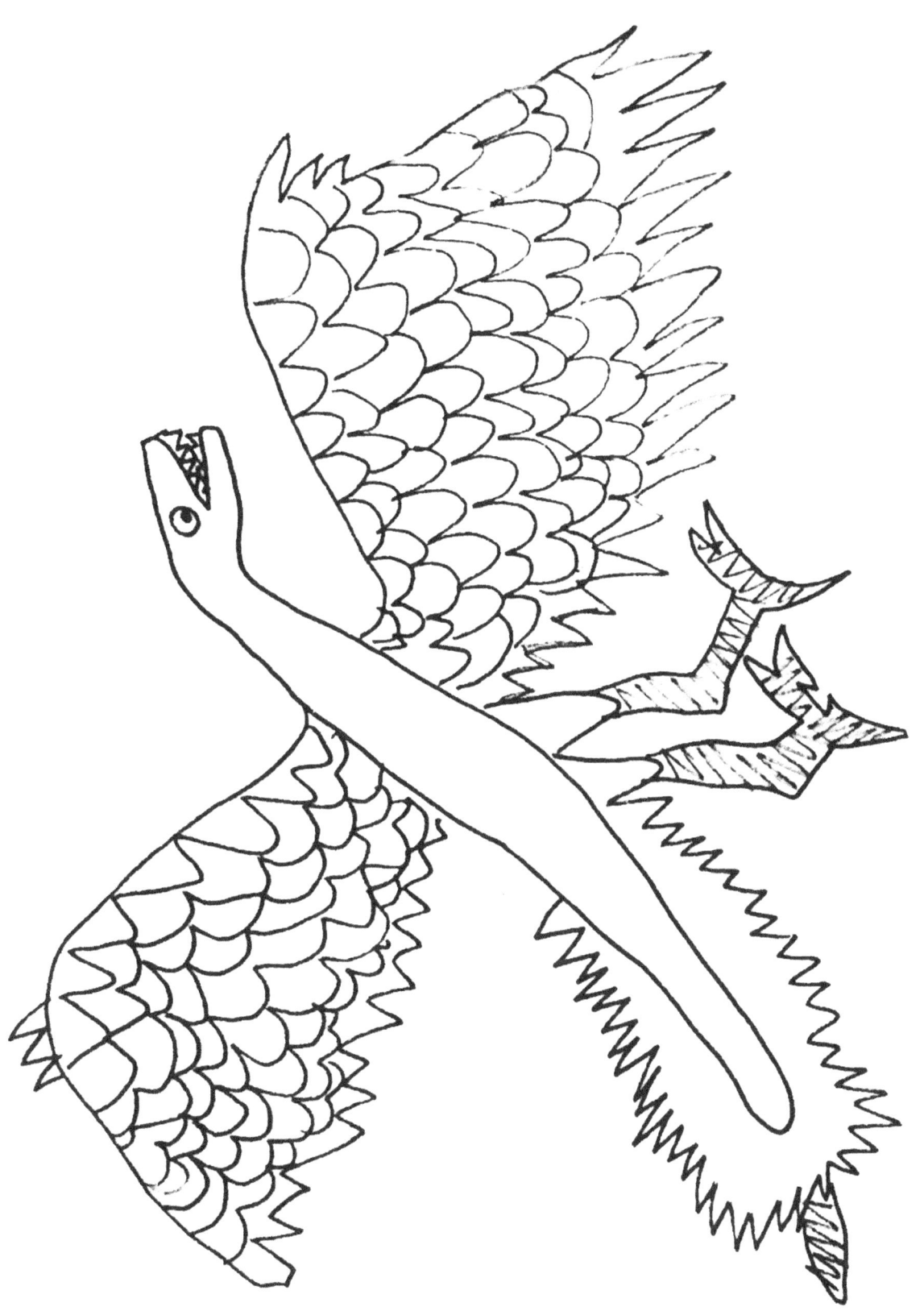

.

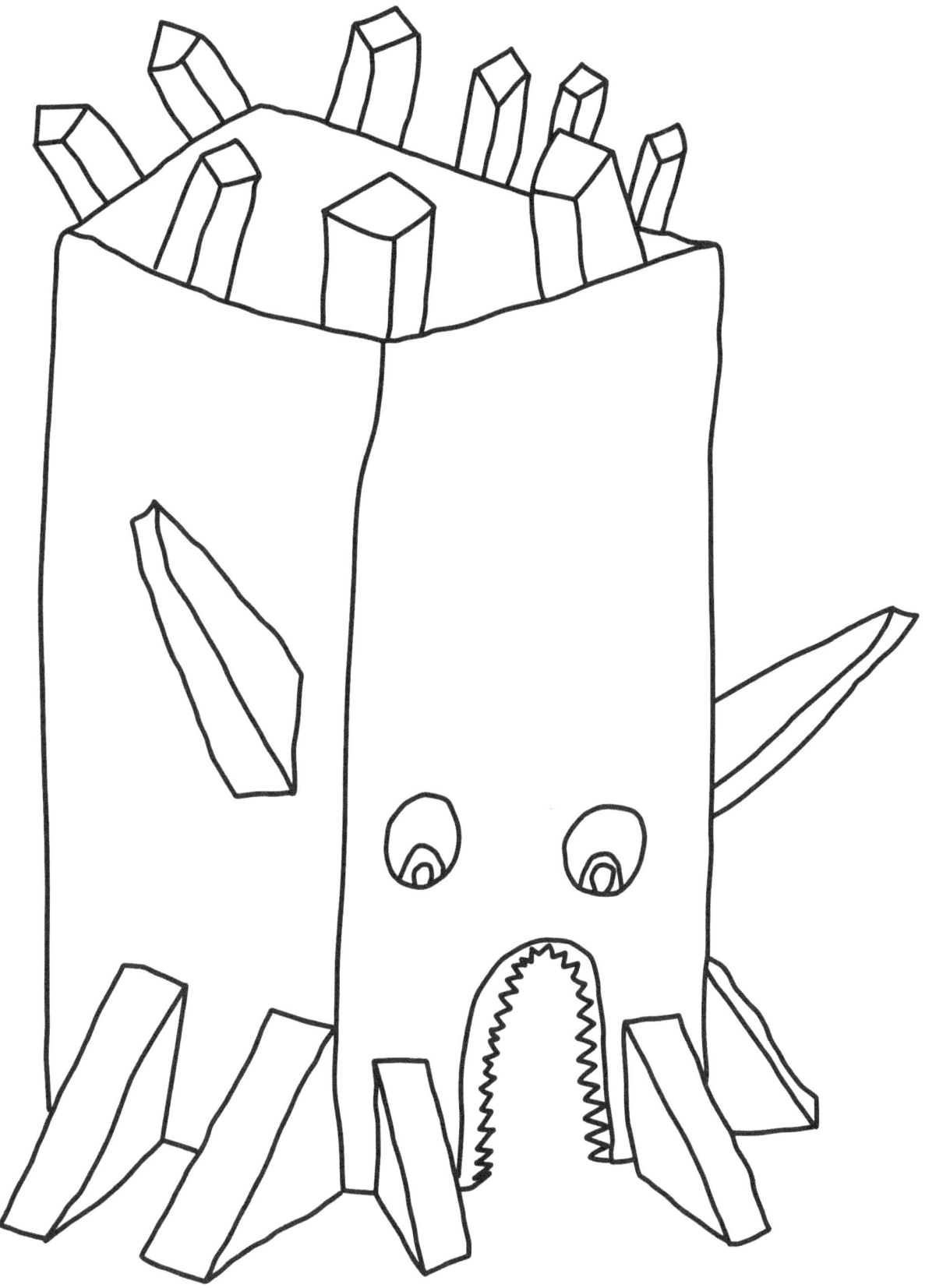

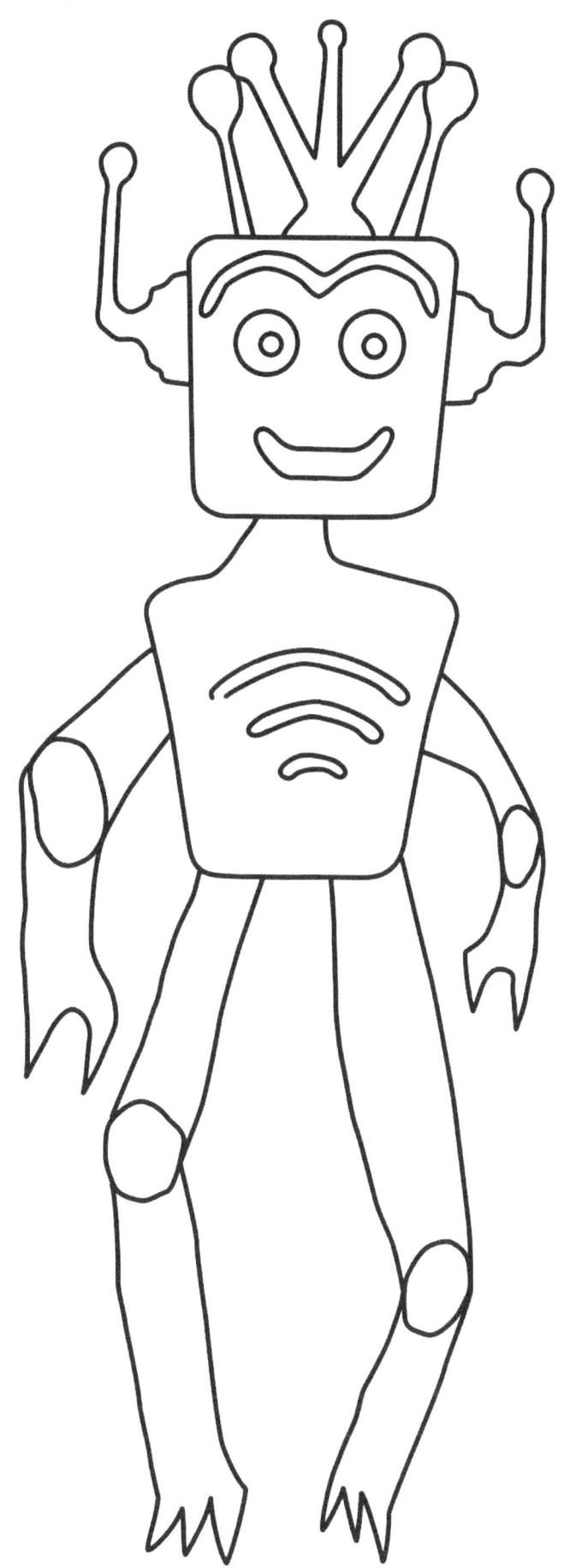

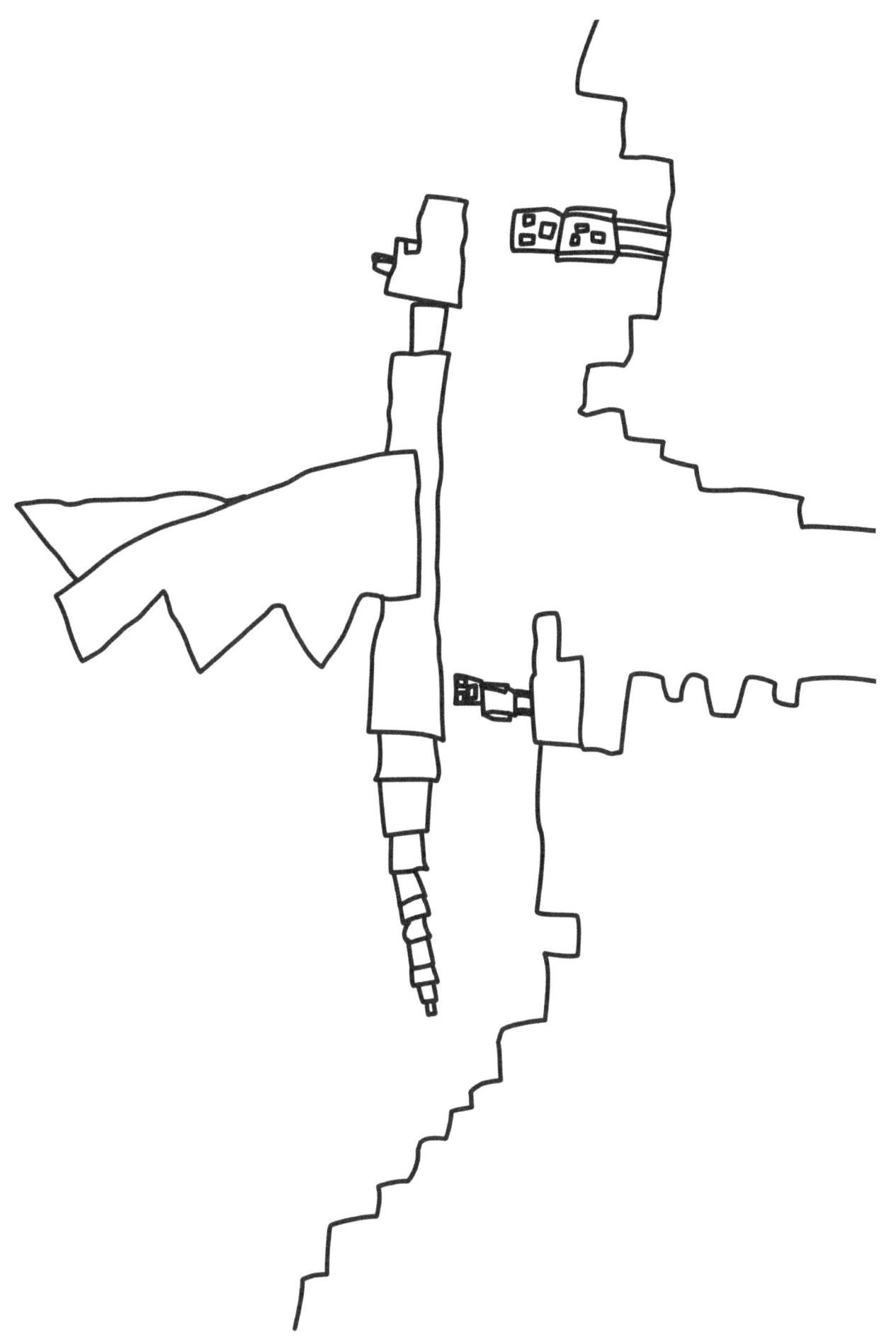

.

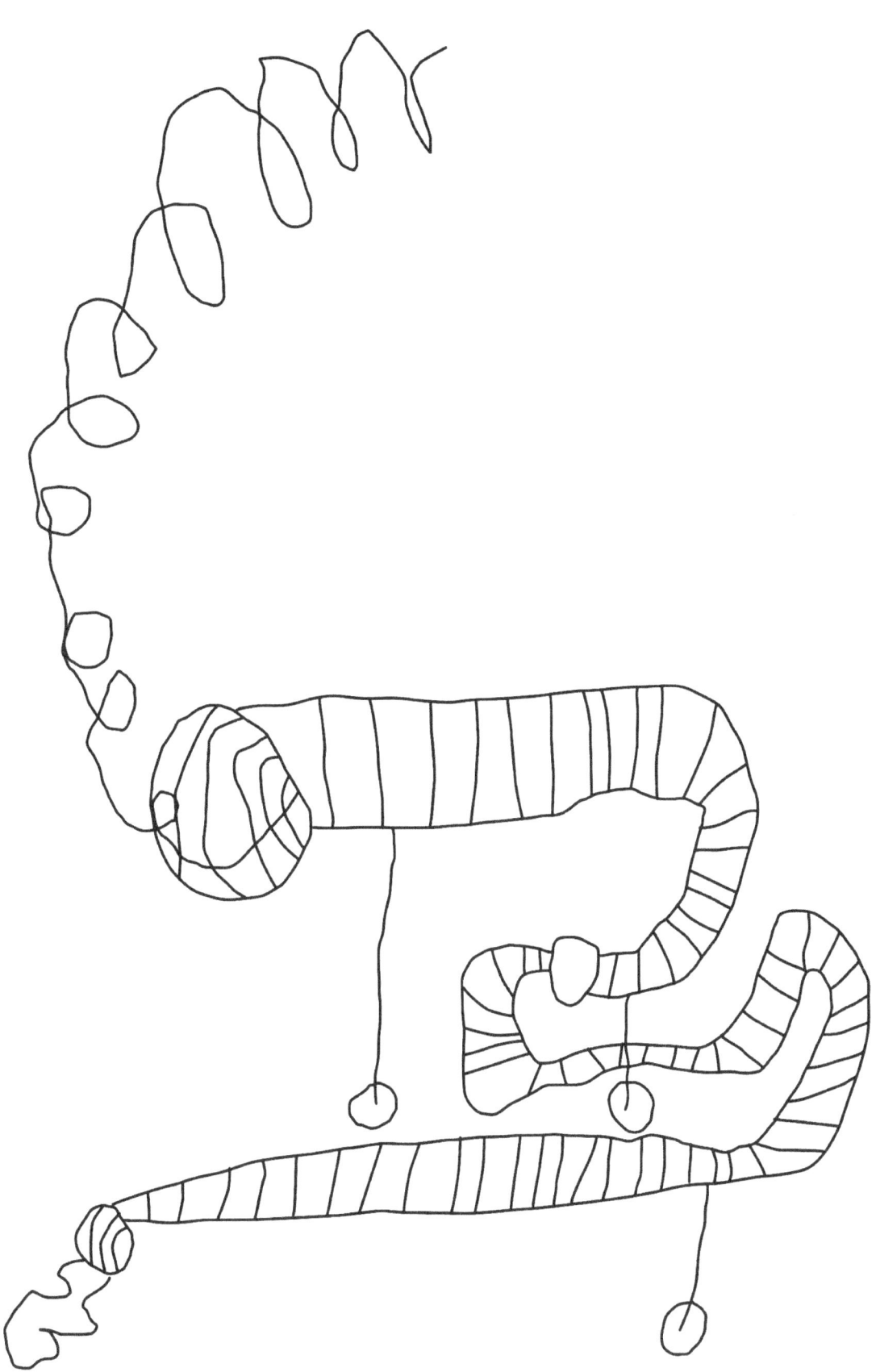

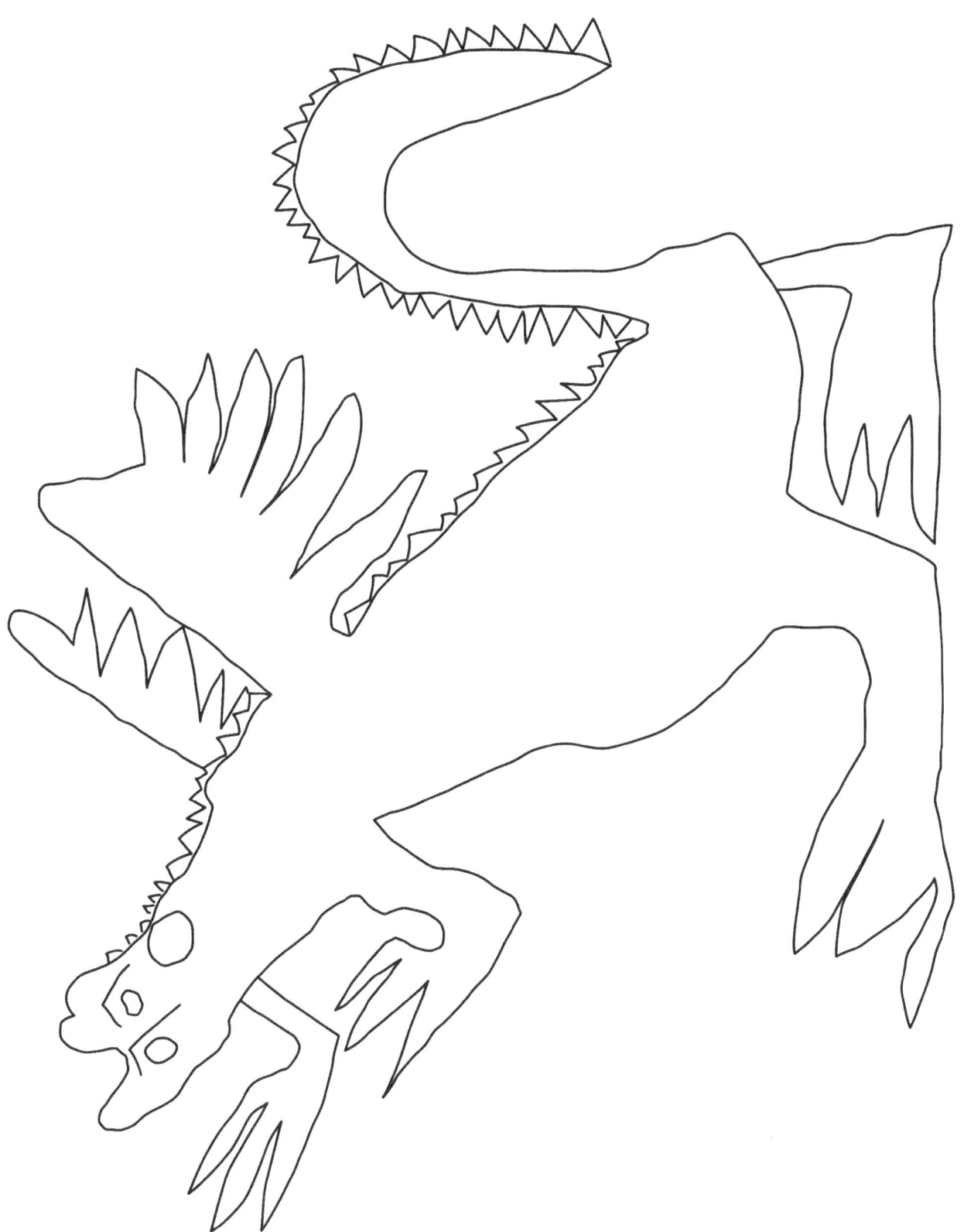

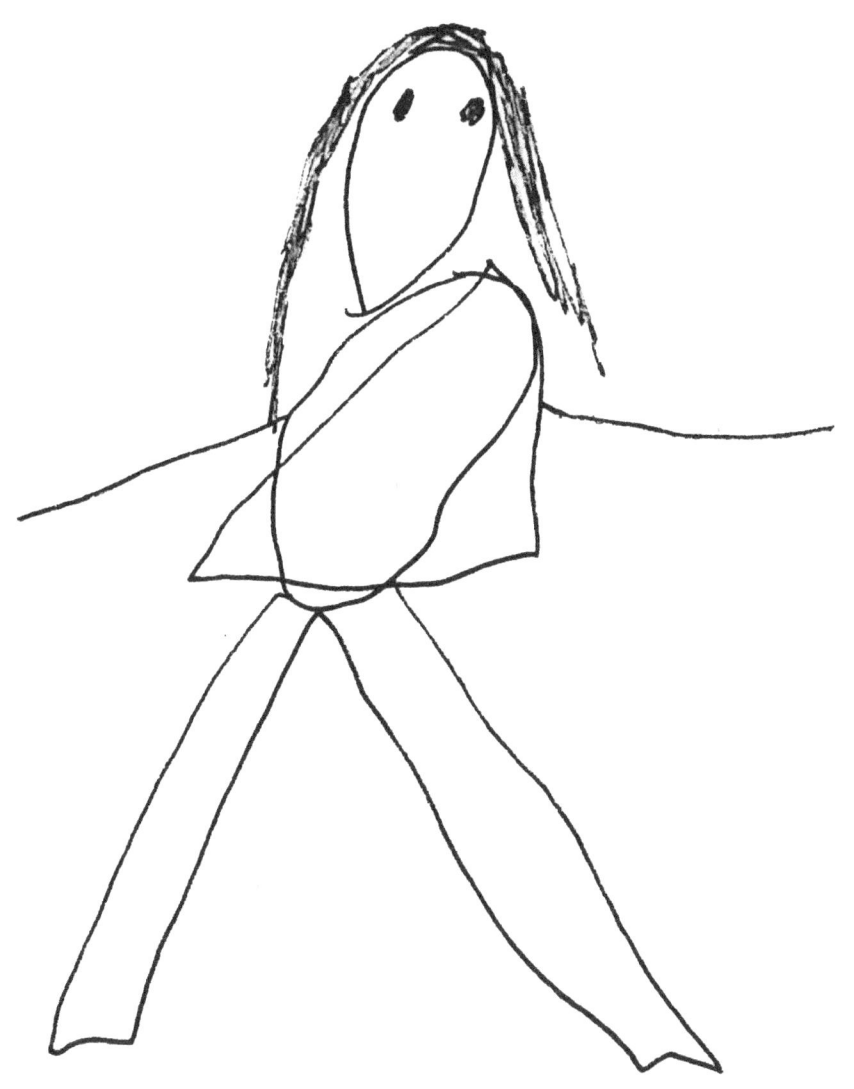

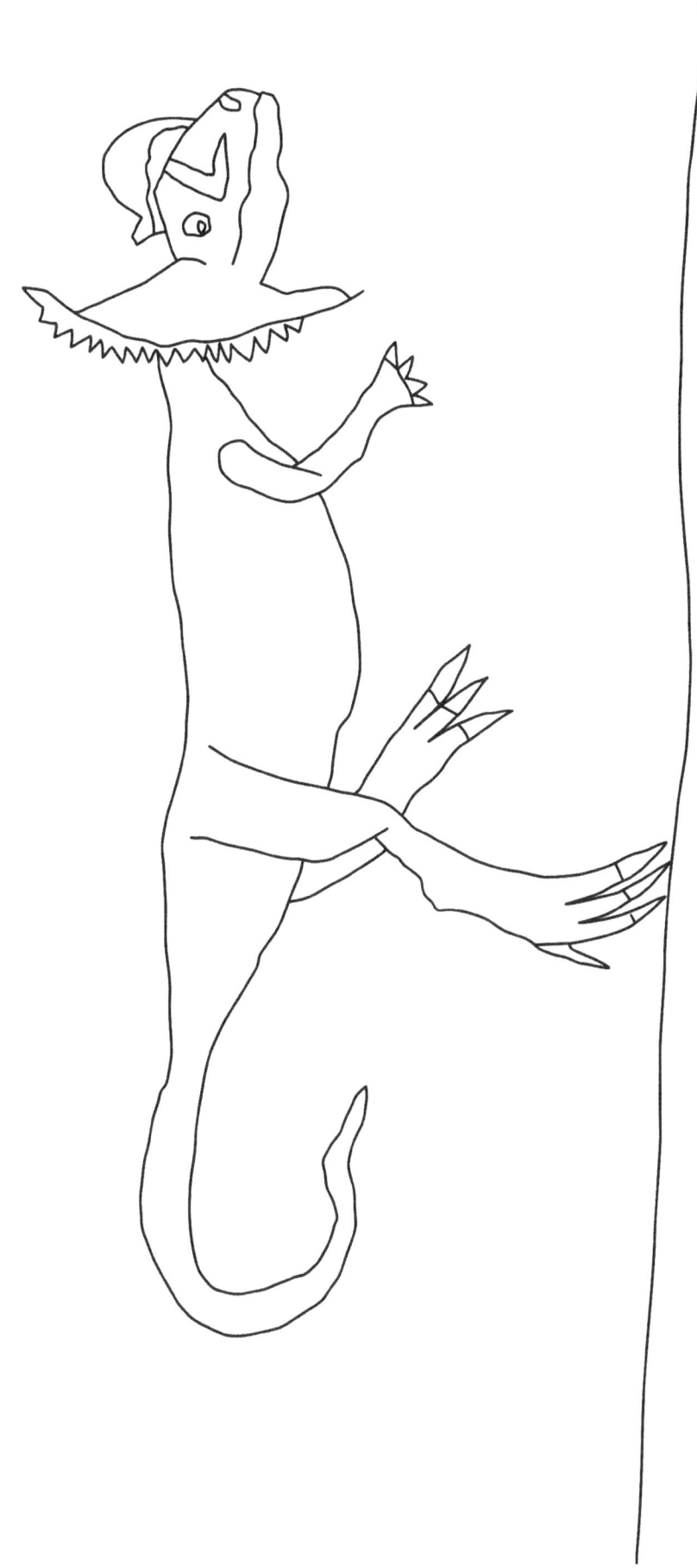

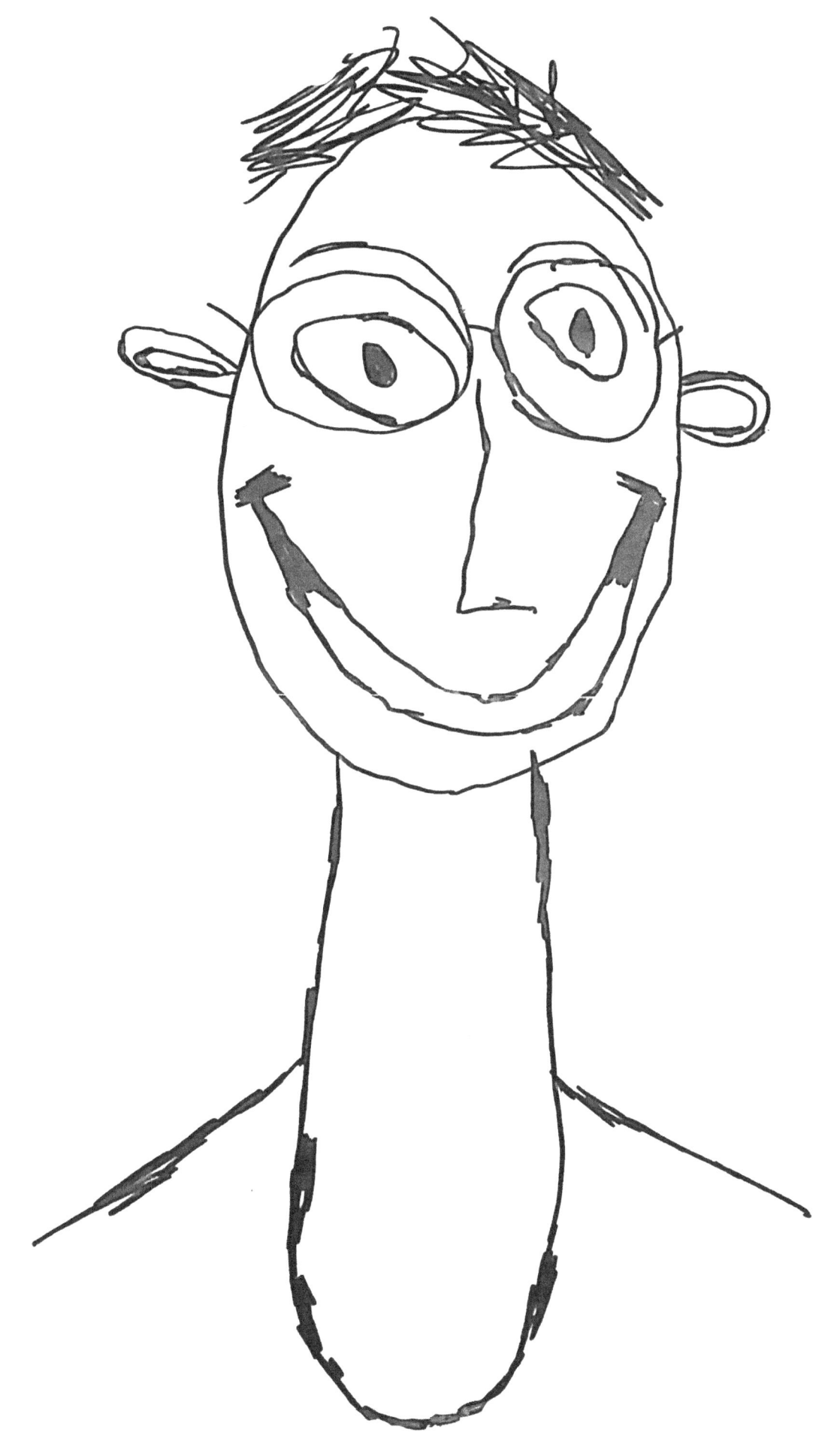

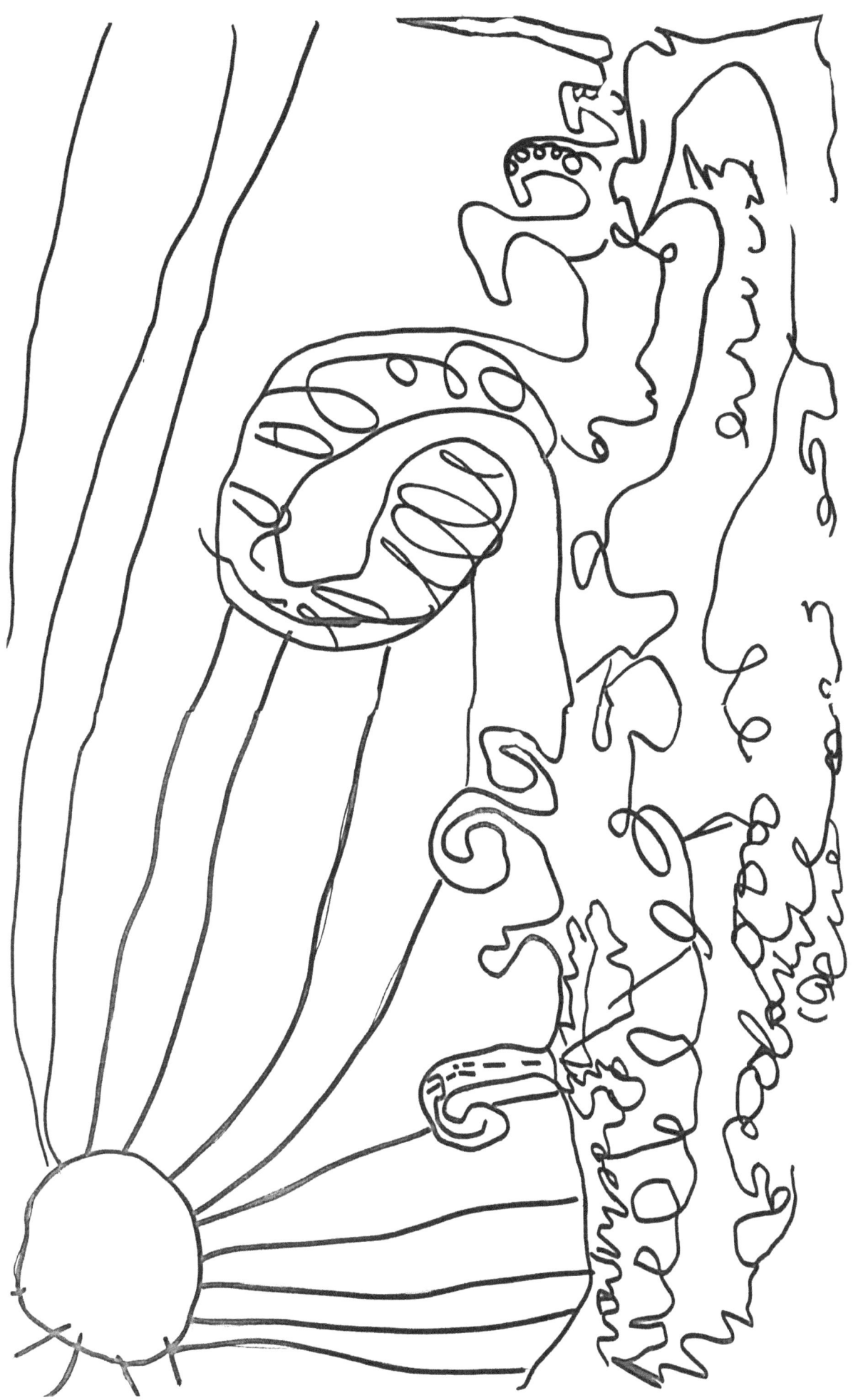

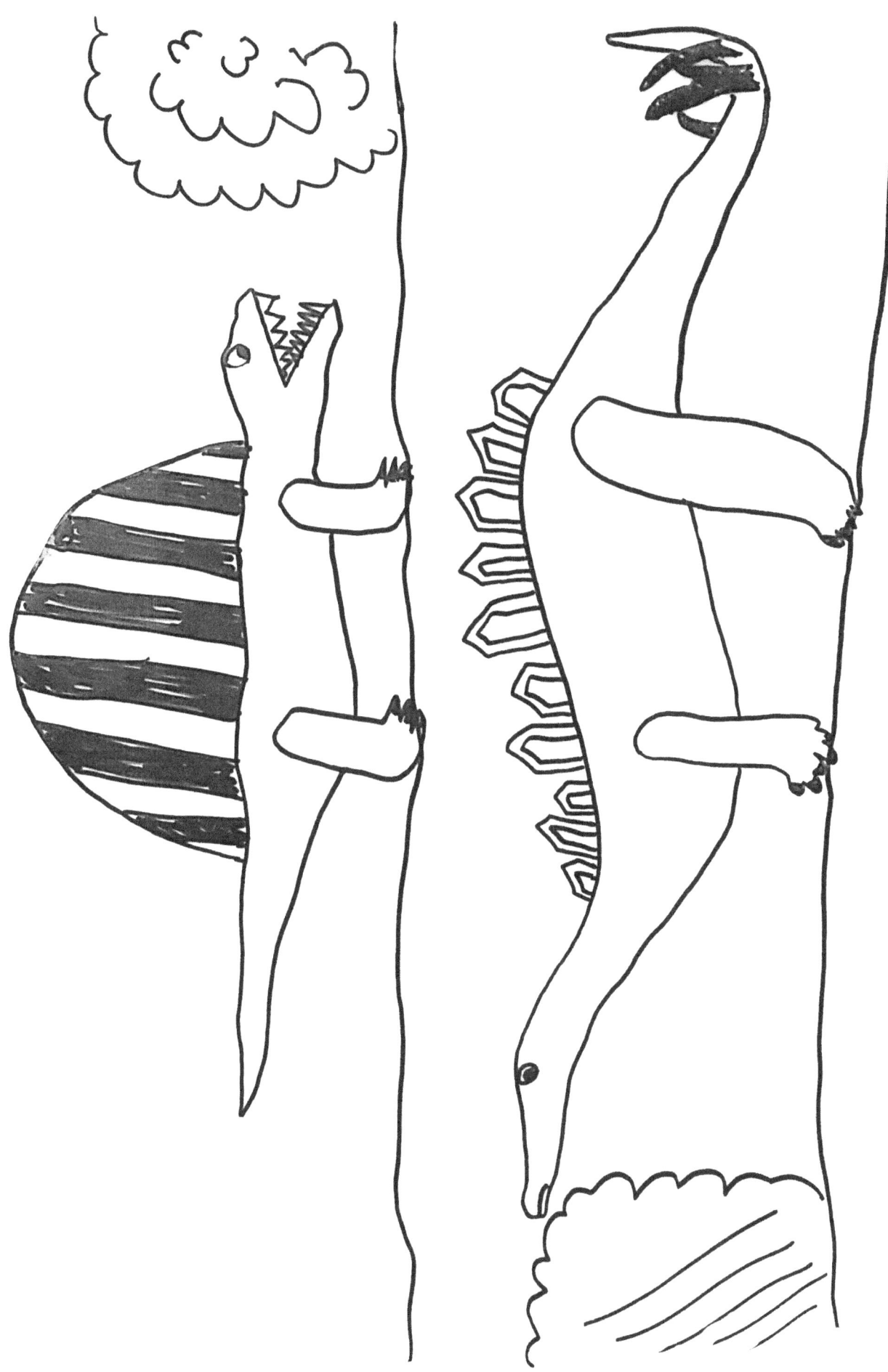

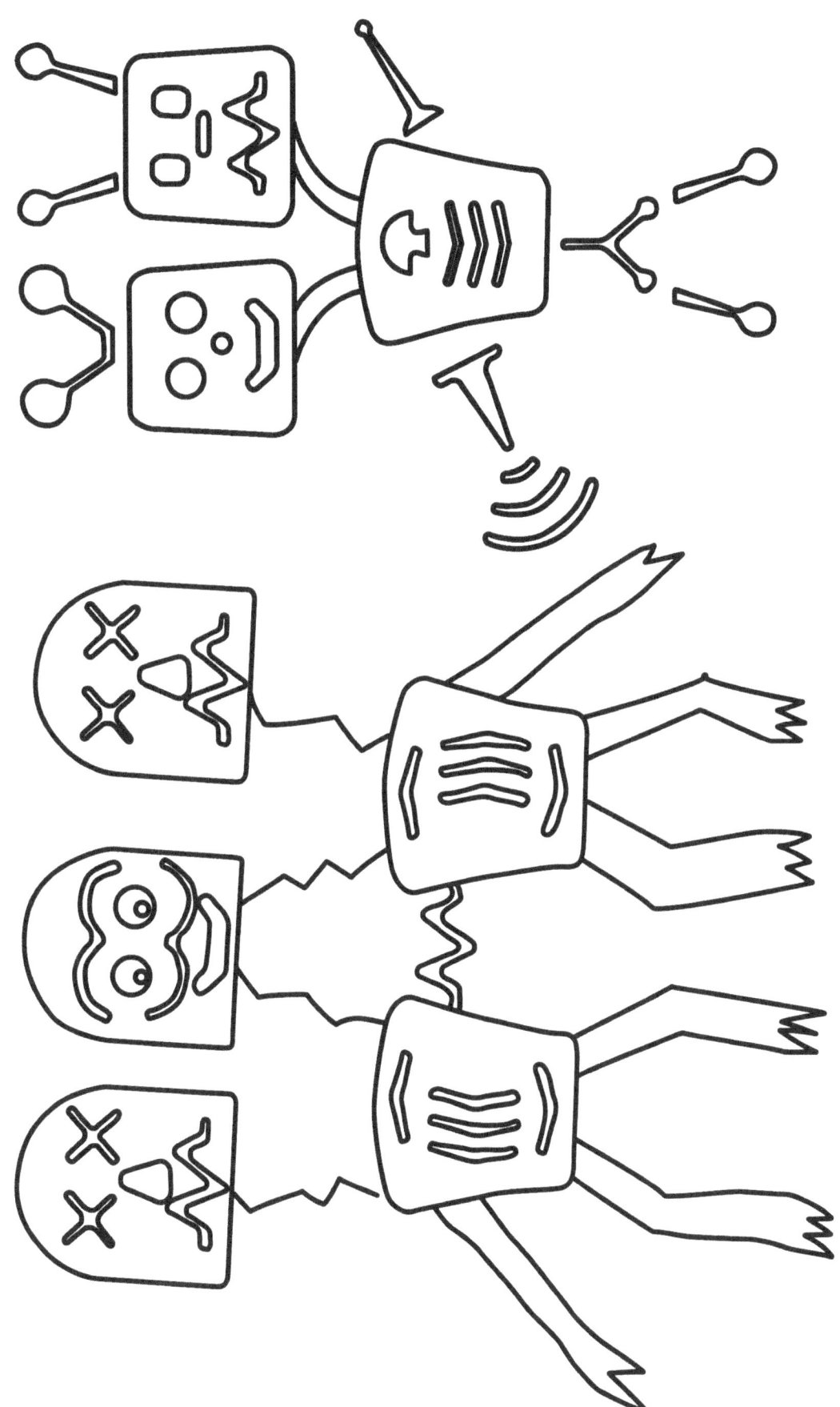

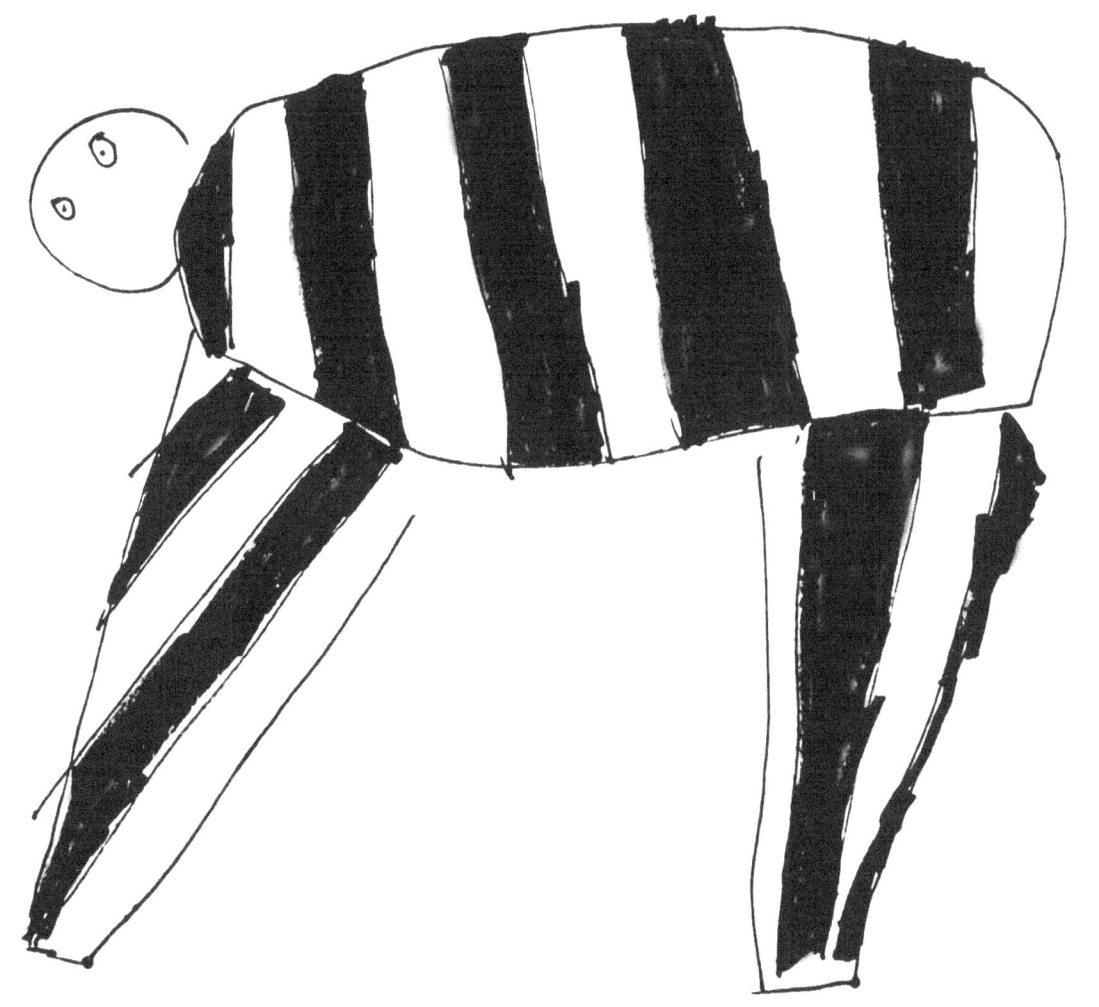

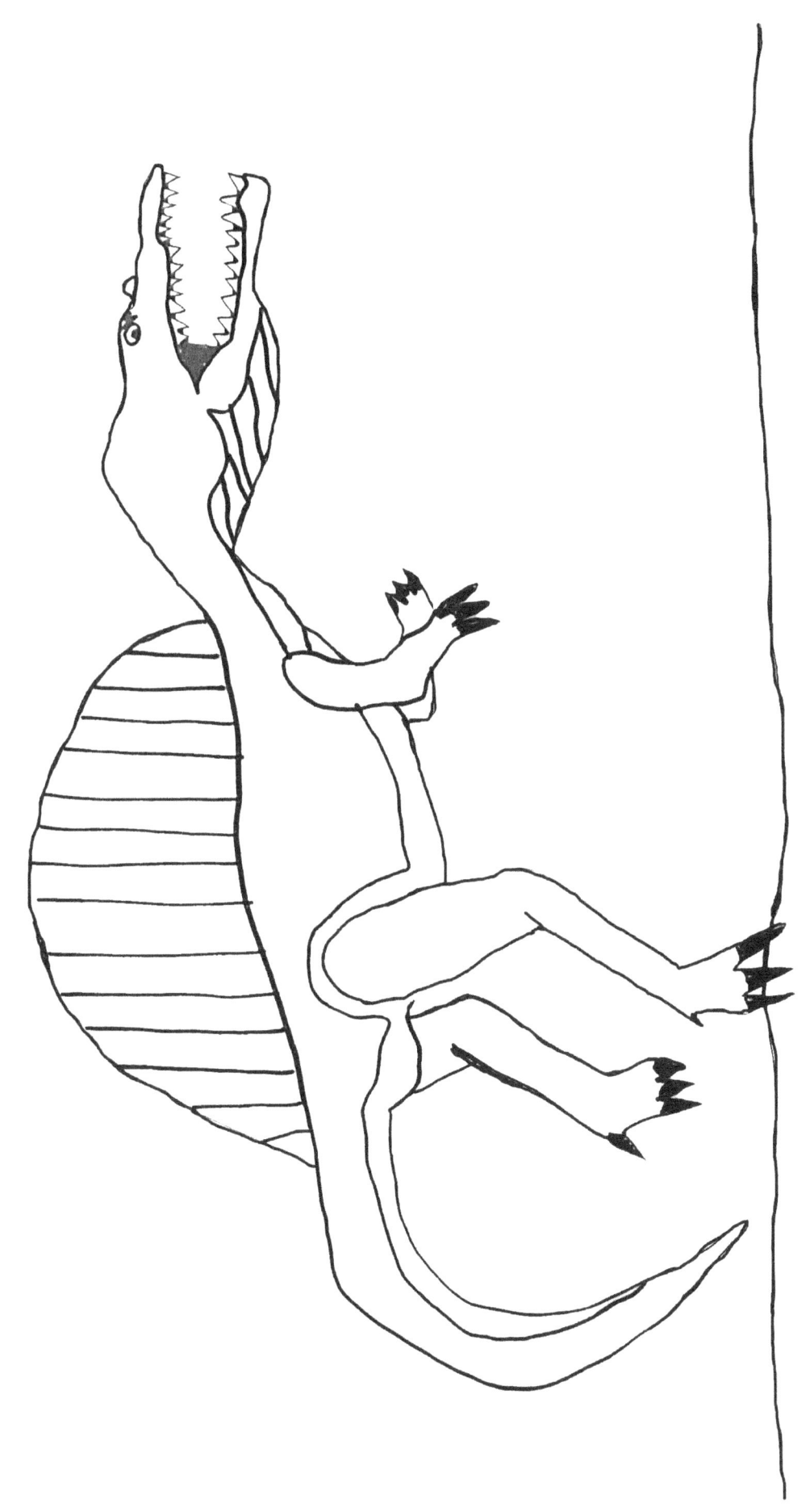

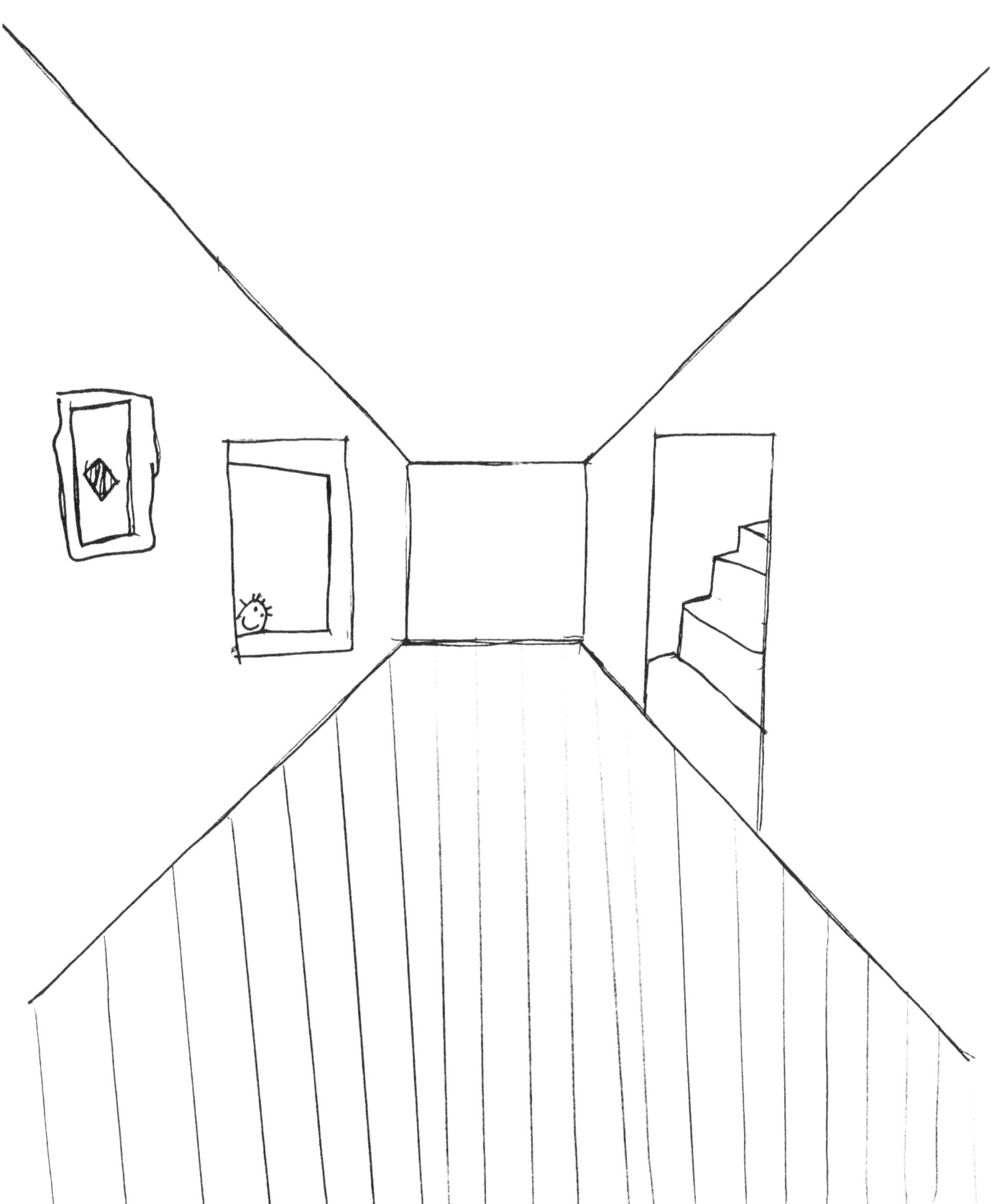

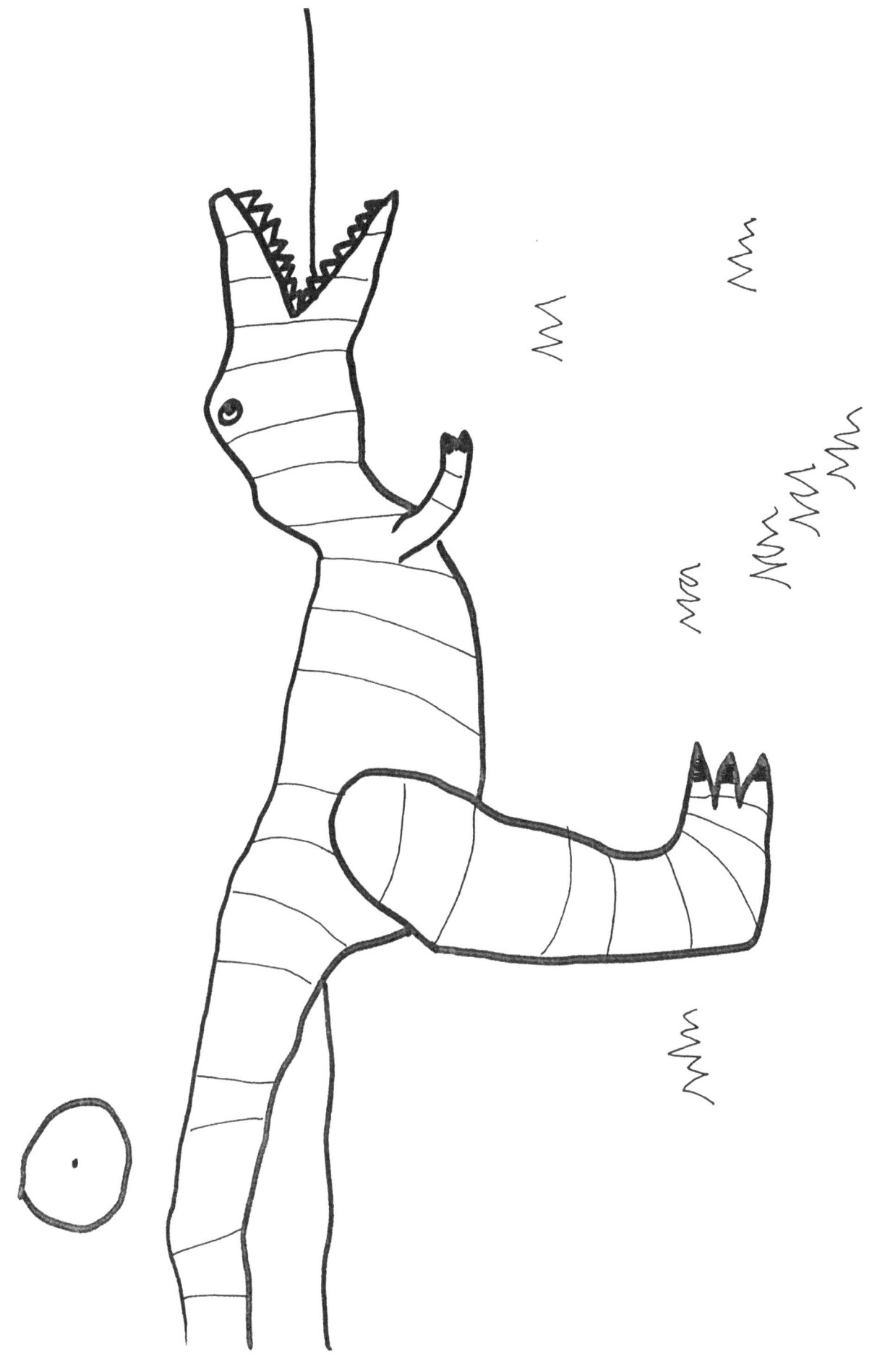

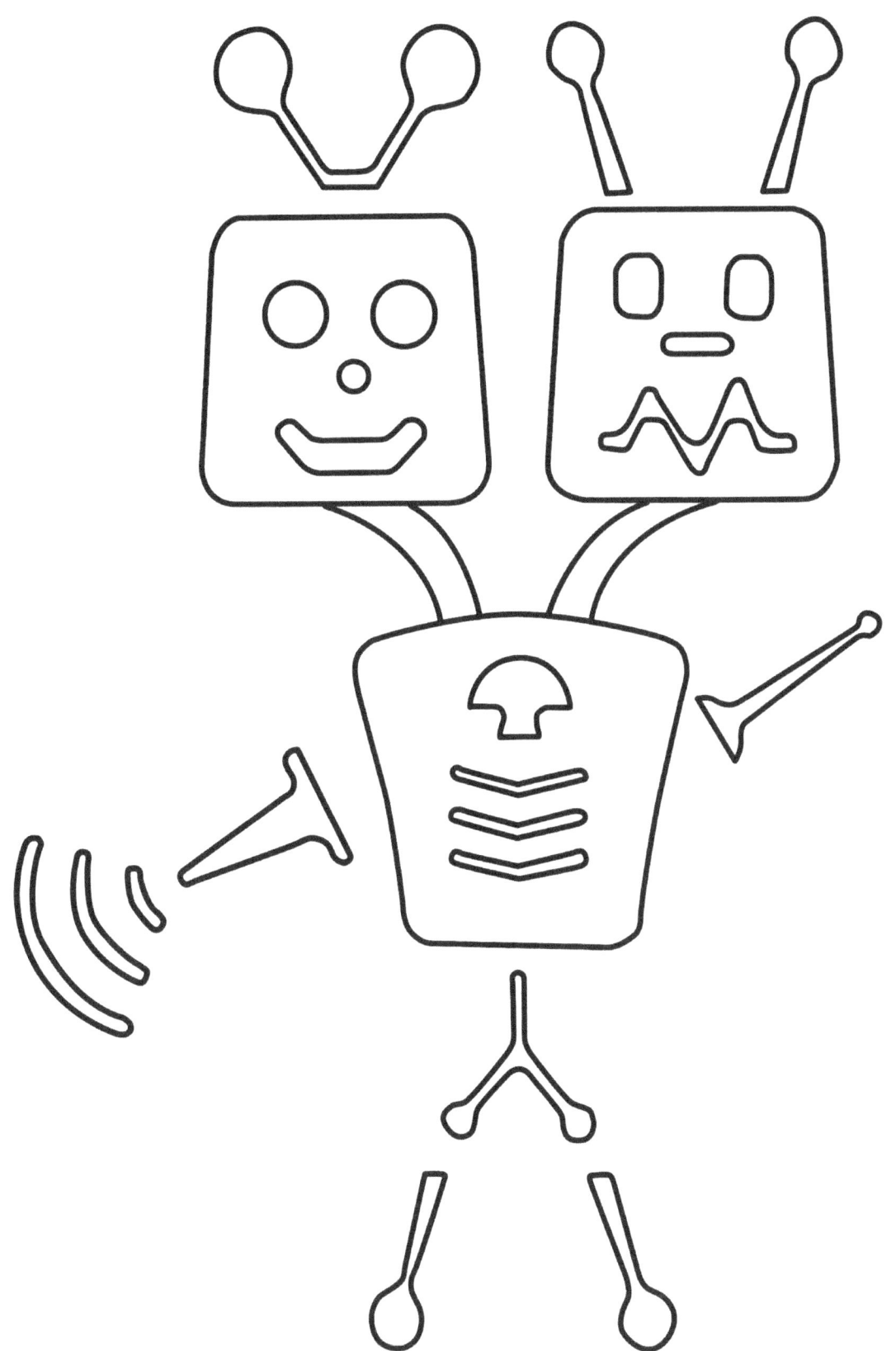

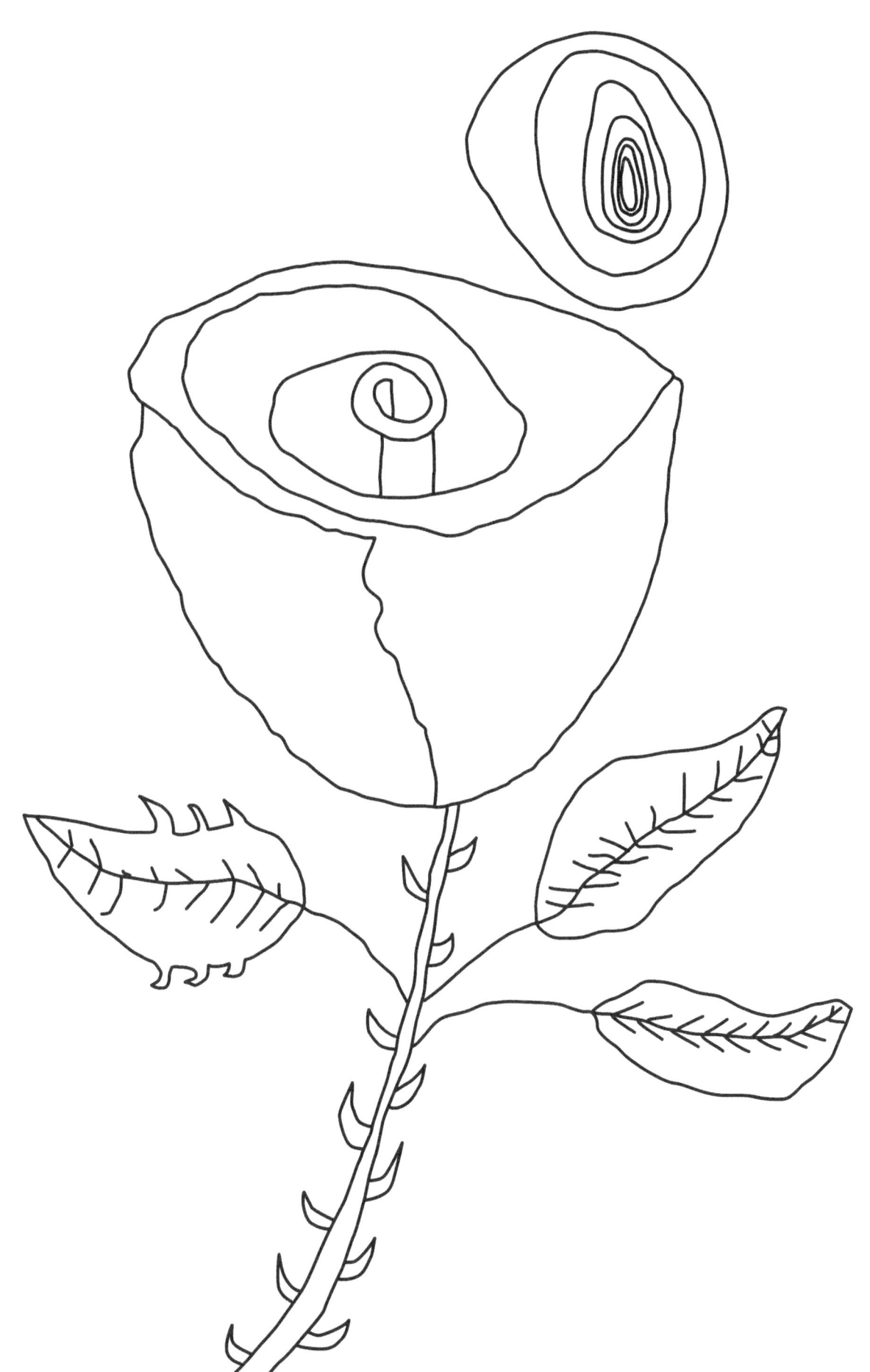

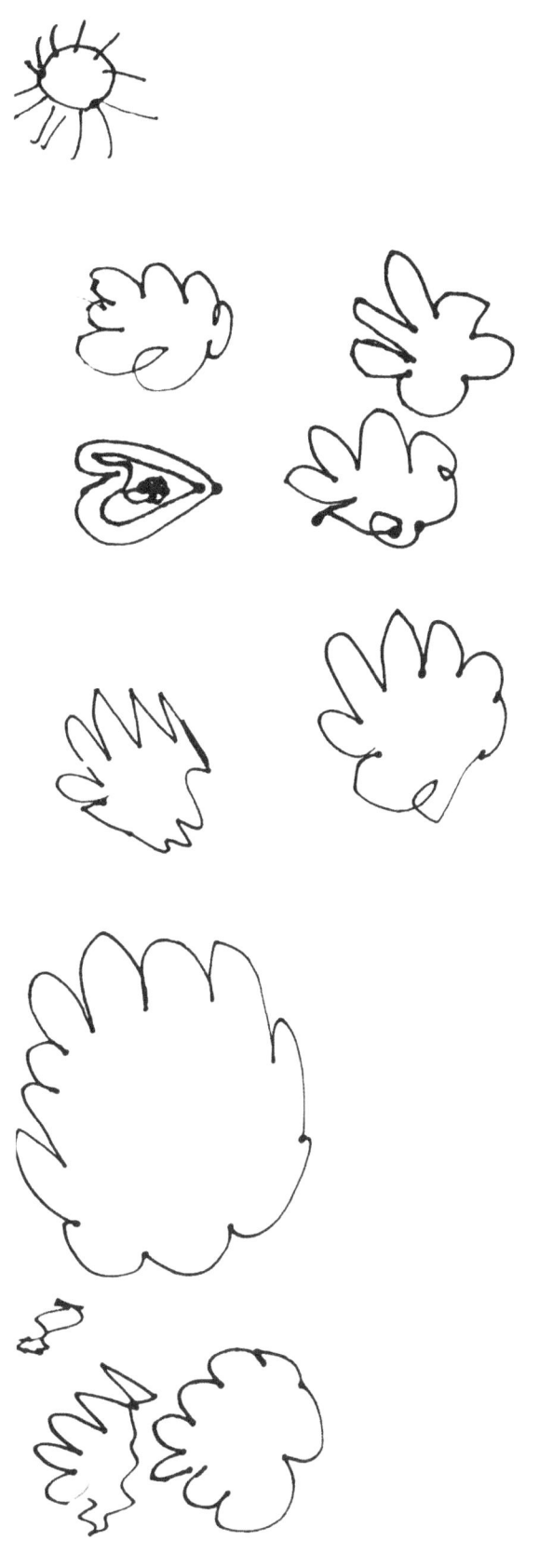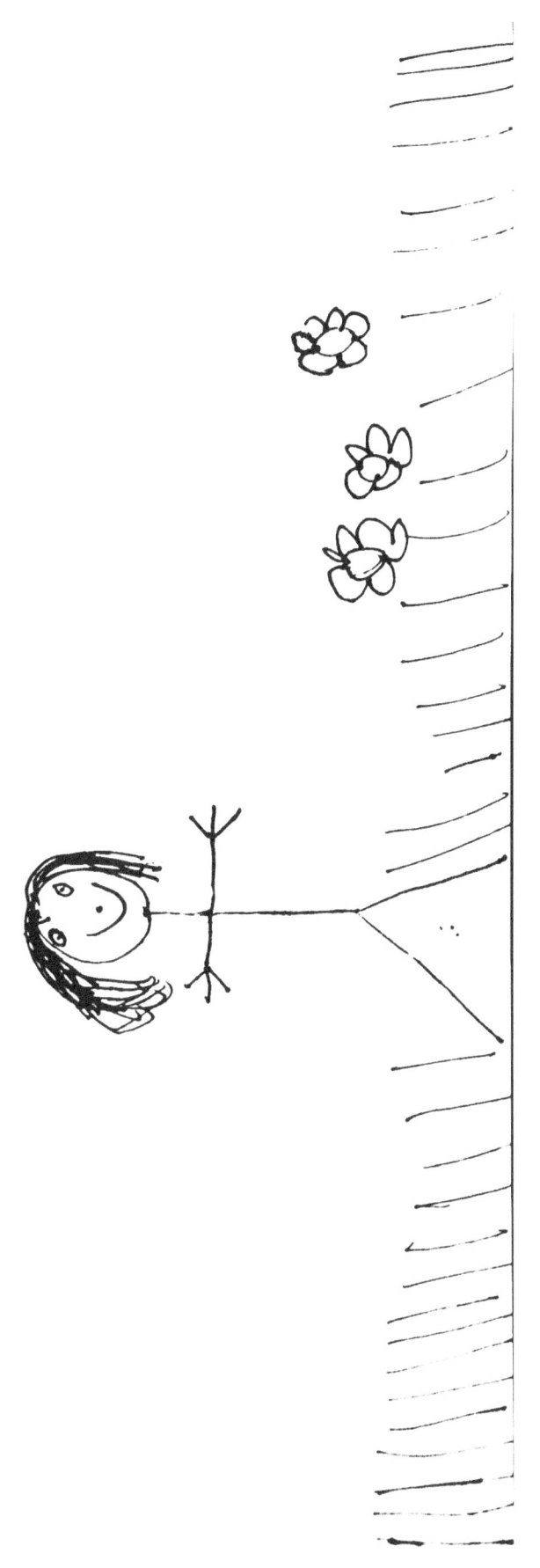

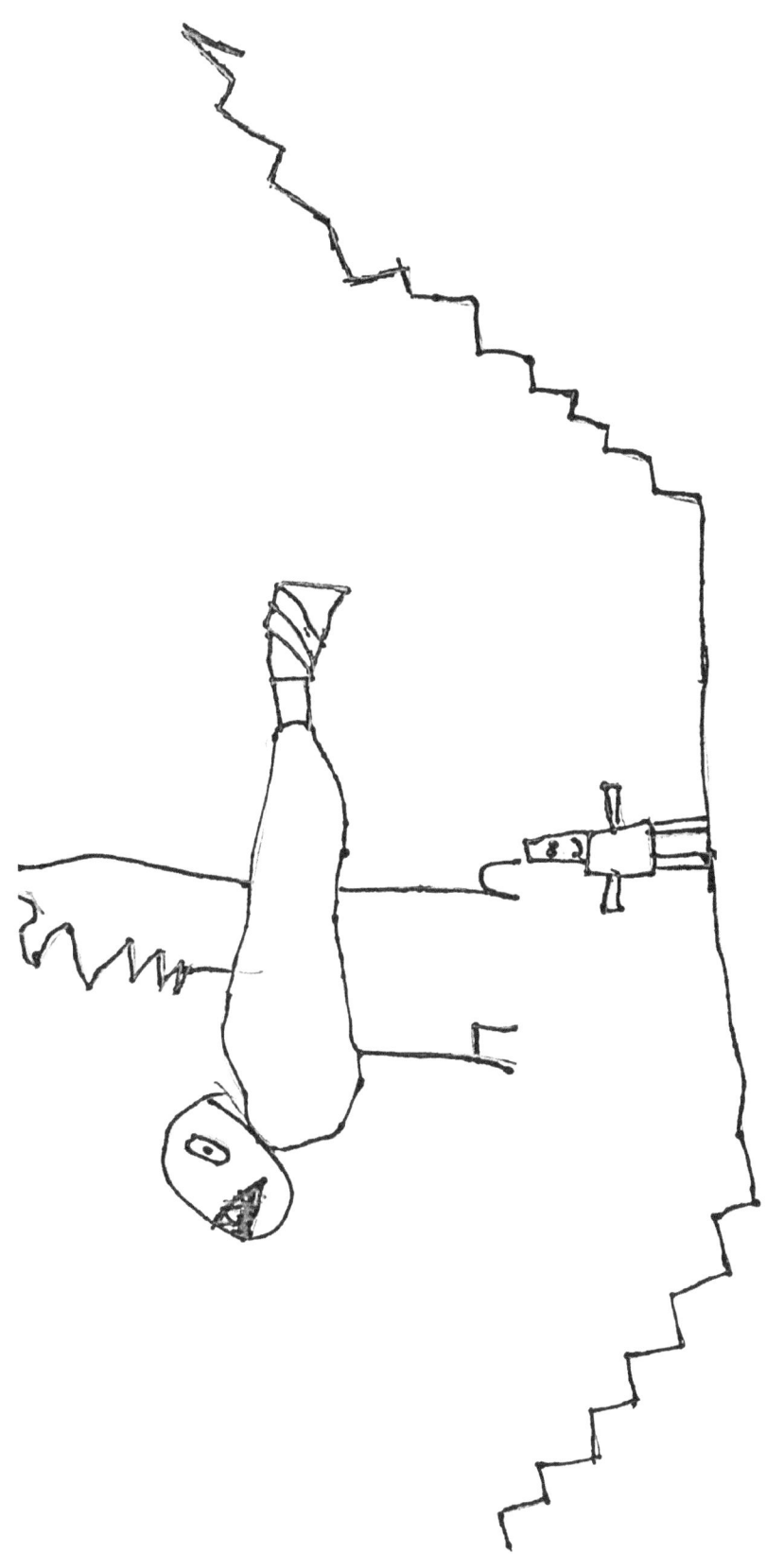

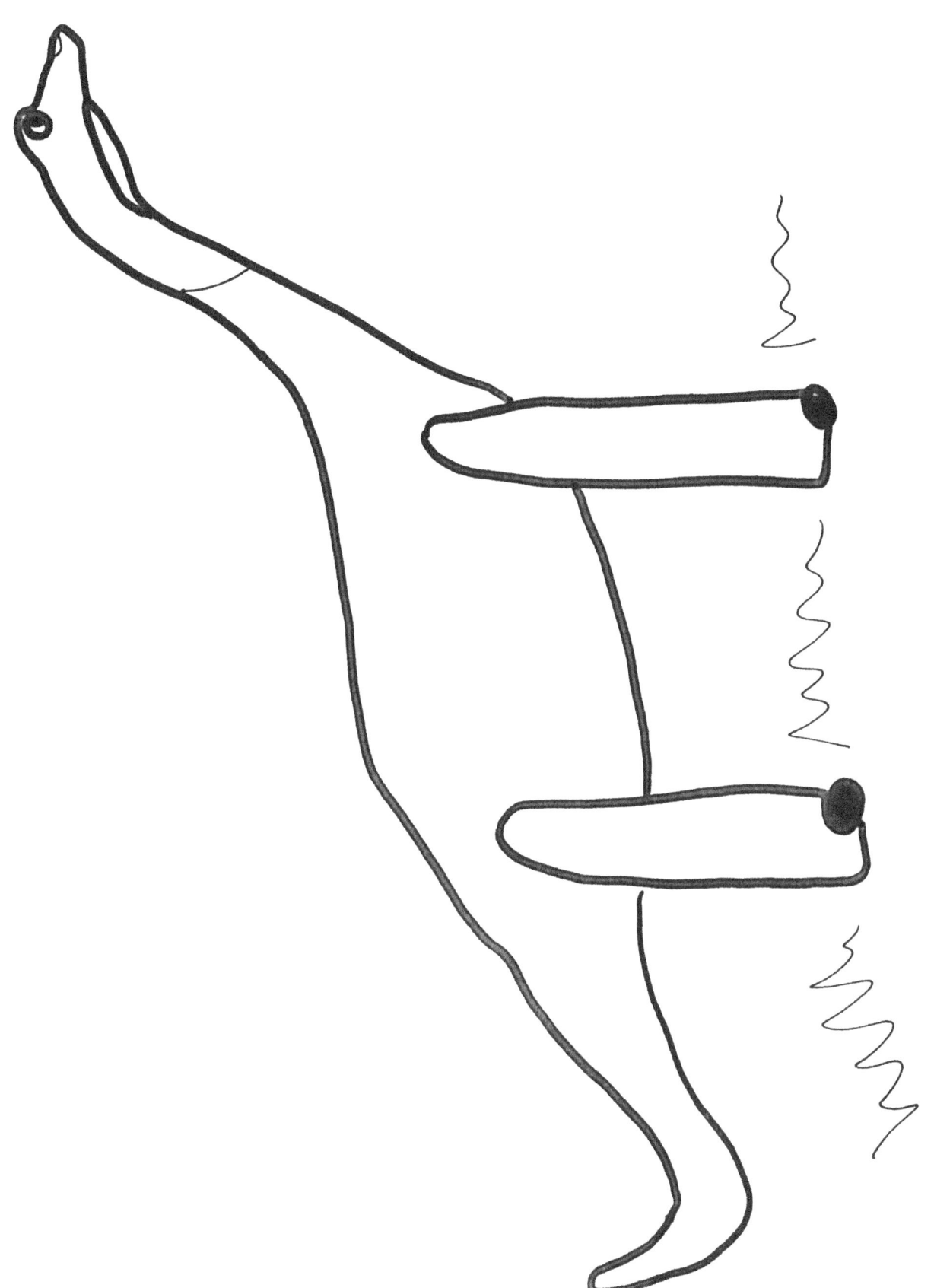

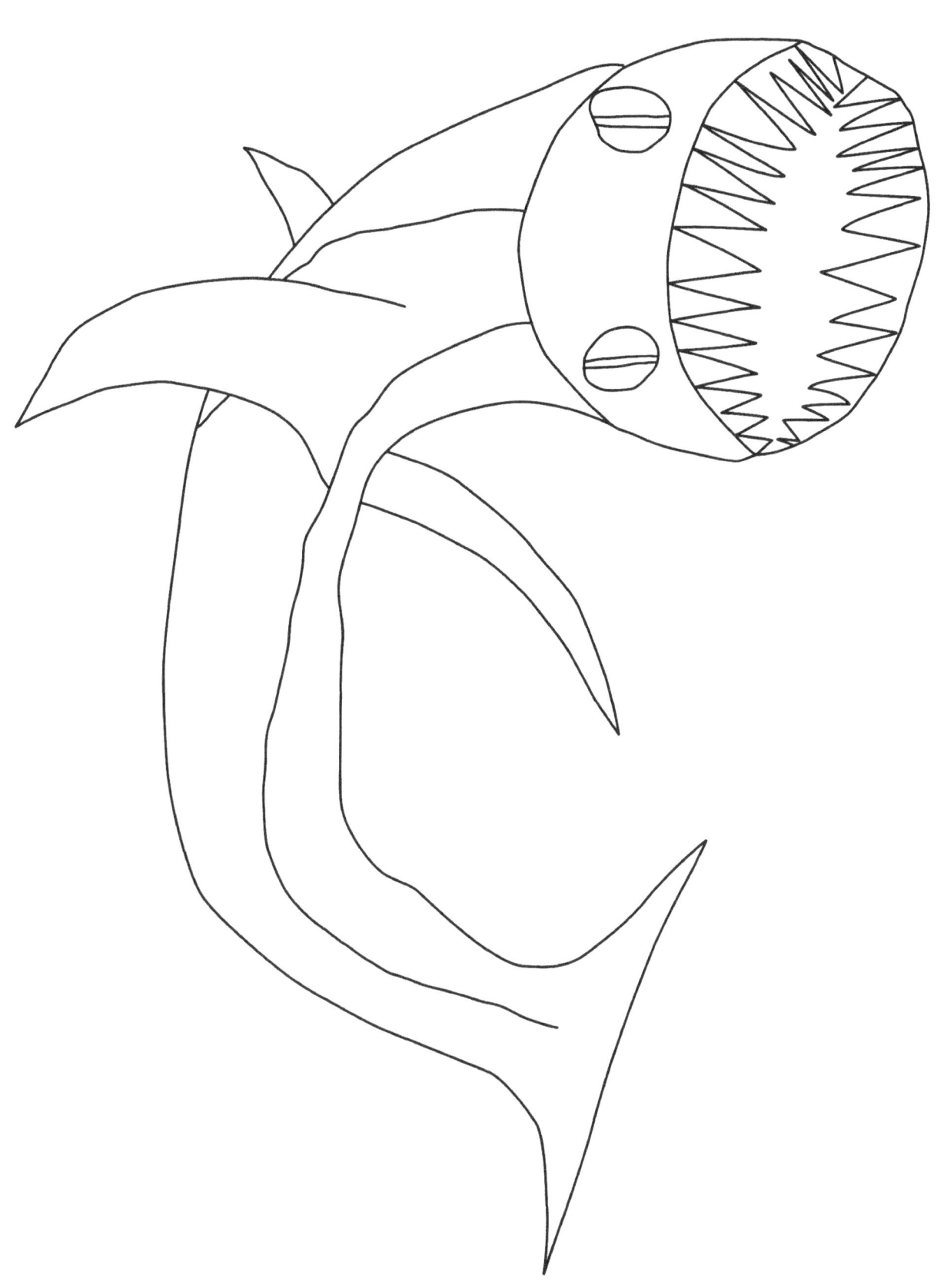

ABOUT THE AUTHORS

Foster (9yrs) and Rowan (7yrs) Weldon are brothers & best friends. They can be found building tree houses, drawing dinosaurs, building huge lego creations, shooting bow & arrows, playing an array of sports, helping their mom & dad around the house or playing with their two younger sisters, Emery (5 yrs.) & Penny (1 yr). Their sister, Emery, also contributed several drawings to this book and spends much of her time dancing and creating all types of artwork.

We hope you enjoy coloring our pages as much as we enjoyed making them!

Other volumes will be coming out soon - and we want you to be a part of them!
Check out our website to find out how you can be in our next coloring book!

www. inspiremecoloringpages.com

CREATIVE CREDIT

The following drawings were created by us while we were studying our techniques using
You Can Draw in 30 Days by Mark Kistler. Its an amazing book and a great one to add to your personal artistic library!
While these are our own versions, we want to give credit to the original artist.

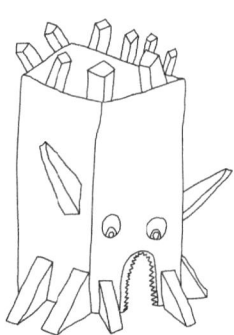 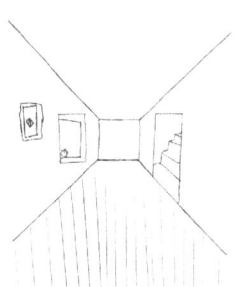 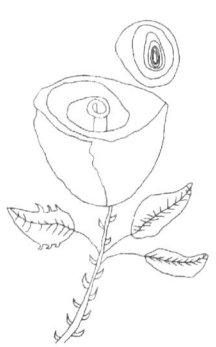

·

www.ingramcontent.com/pod-product-compliance
Lightning Source LLC
Chambersburg PA
CBHW080646180526
45168CB00008B/3325